Celtic Spirituality

Also by Philip Freeman

The Rule of St. Benedict

Celtic Spirituality

An INTRODUCTION to the SACRED WISDOM of the CELTS

Philip Freeman

ST. MARTIN'S
ESSENTIALS
NEW YORK

First published in the United States by St. Martin's Essentials,
an imprint of St. Martin's Publishing Group

www.stmartins.com

Designed by Steven Seighman

Library of Congress Cataloging-in-Publication Data

Names: Freeman, Philip, 1961– editor.
Title: Celtic spirituality : an introduction to the sacred
    wisdom of the Celts / [edited by] Philip Freeman.
Description: First edition. | New York : St. Martin's
    Essentials, 2021. | Includes bibliographical references.
Identifiers: LCCN 2020057507 | ISBN 9781250780201
    (trade paperback) | ISBN 9781250780218 (ebook)
Subjects: LCSH: Celts—Religion. | Mythology, Celtic.
    | Wisdom—Religious aspects. | Celtic literature.
Classification: LCC BL900 .C448 2021 | DDC 299/.1614—dc23
LC record available at https://lccn.loc.gov/2020057507

Our books may be purchased in bulk for promotional,
educational, or business use. Please contact your local bookseller
or the Macmillan Corporate and Premium Sales Department at
1-800-221-7945, extension 5442, or by email at
MacmillanSpecialMarkets@macmillan.com.

First Edition: 2021

10   9   8   7   6   5   4   3   2   1

Contents

Introduction

It was the Dagda who distributed the
síd mounds of Ireland to the Tuatha Dé
Danaan—to Lug, Ogma, and all the rest. But
he kept the best of síd mounds, the great tomb
at Newgrange, for himself.

—from "The Taking of the *Síd* Mound"

Drive north of Dublin in the dark morning hours of the winter solstice past the tidy suburban homes and modern shopping malls and you will soon come to the green banks of the River Boyne. Park your car at the Brú na Bóinne Visitor Centre and make your way across the river and up the path to a curving wall of white stones barely visible in the faint glow of the coming dawn. Walk past the intricate, swirling decorations carved ages ago on the huge rock by the entrance and then under the massive stone lintel with its roof-box opening facing southeast above you. Walk in reverent silence down the long, dark passageway to the central chamber that was old centuries before the Egyptians built the pyramids at Giza. Feel the cold of the ancient stones against your hands and hear the sound of your own heart beating in the darkness.

Then turn around.

Down the long passageway and through the distant hole above the lintel you will see a beam of light from the rising sun piercing the shadows of the tomb and scattering the darkness all around you.

For more than five thousand years the great tomb of Newgrange on the River Boyne has been a sacred space and an important part of Irish spiritual beliefs. For the Neolithic farmers who built it, it was a place aligned with the movements of the heavens to honor their ancestors and gods. For the Celts who arrived after them, it was a place of ancient magic, the home of the mystical Tuatha Dé Danaan, and a doorway into the dangers and delights of the Otherworld. For Christians after the arrival of St. Patrick, it was a reminder that the old gods still dwelled in the land of Ireland—divinities who were as much a part of the spiritual landscape of the island as the green hills and flowing rivers.

The Celts of ancient Europe stretched from Ireland and Britain to Spain, France (called Gaul in early times), northern Italy, central Europe, and into the lands of Galatia in Anatolia. They were a thriving culture that, while never united as a single empire, were a source of looming danger and endless fascination to the Greeks and Romans of the Mediterranean world. Julius Caesar crushed the Celts of Gaul in the first century BCE and Roman armies subdued other Celtic lands, but traditional Celtic beliefs survived for centuries afterward, even under occupation. In Ireland, a Celtic land never conquered by the legions, the old ways of the gods and druids lasted until well after the arrival of Christian missionaries. Indeed, in some ways they survive still today.

Sadly, so much about the spiritual world of the ancient Celts has been lost to us. What does remain are tales told from long ago written on faded manuscript pages, along with a few rituals, magic spells, poems, and prayers that give us at least a glimpse into a forgotten time. In this small book it has been my goal to give modern readers a selection of the best authentic Celtic stories and sources that remain from both pre-Christian and early Christian spiritual life, so that you may discover them for yourself and listen to the ancient voices of the Celts that can still speak to us today.

A NOTE ON THE READINGS

The passages and stories that follow were written over the course of many centuries. The earliest were recorded by sometimes hostile Greeks and Romans observing the Celts from the outside and writing about them in Greek or Latin, but most come from Celtic authors themselves writing about their own lives and traditions in Gaulish, Latin, Irish, or Welsh. I've translated some of them word for word from the original languages, but many are paraphrases or retellings based closely on the native sources and condensed for brevity's sake. In all of them I've tried to preserve the style, flavor, and wonder of the original tales.

Celtic Spirituality

The Gods and Goddesses of the Ancient Celts

Only scattered fragments remain of the rich and complex religious traditions of the early Celtic tribes. Archaeology is telling us more each year about the physical remains of Celtic religion, but we are still forced to rely mostly on secondhand observations by Greek and Roman authors who were often hostile to the Celts and who usually substituted the names of their own Greek and Roman gods for native Celtic names. But if we do our best to see beyond the bias of these classical writers, we can glimpse a fascinating world of countless gods and goddesses who inhabited and illuminated every corner of ancient Celtic life.

The most important god of the Gauls is Mercury. There are images of him throughout the land. He is said to be the inventor of all human arts, the guide for every path and journey, and the god in charge of trade and commerce.

After Mercury, the most important gods are Apollo,

Mars, Jupiter, and Minerva. These gods are in charge of the same areas of life as among other peoples—Apollo cures diseases, Minerva oversees crafts, Jupiter rules the skies, and Mars is the god of war.

Before a great battle the Gauls will often dedicate the spoils of the enemy to Mars. If they win, they sacrifice all the animals they capture to the god and collect the other captured goods in a single place among their tribe. You may often see these objects piled up in a sacred spot among whatever tribe you visit. It is most rare that anyone will dare to disturb these spoils or steal from them. If someone does, they are tortured and punished in the most horrible ways imaginable.

The Gods of Darkness

As with many spiritual traditions from around the world, ancient Celtic religion acknowledged a dark side to balance the light. This aspect of Celtic beliefs was emphasized by many Greeks and Romans who wanted to portray the Celts as savages, but to deny its existence altogether is equally dishonest. As the Romans themselves honored their own gods of the underworld, the ancient Celts acknowledged the necessary shadows of life, going so far as to place their own origins in a world of darkness.

The Gauls all say that they are descended from a common father, Dis, the god of the dark underworld. The druids confirm this in their teachings. Because of this belief they measure time by the passing of nights, not days. Birthdays and the beginnings of months and years all start at night.

The Twin Gods
of the Sea

One of the earliest stories we have of Celtic gods come from a frag-ment of a Greek historian named Timaeus who lived in Sicily in the early third century BCE, just after the time of Alexander the Great. The work of Timaeus itself does not survive, but pieces of it were pre-served in later authors. In his history written for a Greek audience, he tells of a Celtic myth about twin gods who came to Celts from the sea, probably to the wild shores of the Atlantic Ocean in Gaul. Like most Greek and Roman authors, he substitutes familiar gods and names from Greek mythology, such as the twins Castor and Pollux, known as the Dioscori ("Sons of Zeus"). Behind this short fragment must lie a rich and fascinating Celtic myth, but it is lost to us forever.

Historians of old tell of the Celts who lived on the shore of the Ocean who honored the Dioscori above all of their gods. There is an ancient tradition among them that these two gods came to them from the sea.

Ancient Gaulish Animal Magic

The world of nature was always important in Celtic religious beliefs and animals were celebrated prominently in Celtic myths and religious practices from the earliest times, often as links between the divine world and our own.

Two stories of sacred birds from ancient Gaul are recorded by Greek writers. The first is from a third-century BCE historian named Eudoxus from the Greek island of Rhodes, while the second comes a century later from a traveler named Artemidorus from the city of Ephesus in Asia Minor. In both cases the original texts have been lost, but fragments are quoted in later, skeptical writers.

Eudoxus says the following about the Celts. Believe it if you want or ignore it if you think it too fanciful.

When clouds of locusts swarm over their country and begin to eat their crops, the Celts offer certain prayers and offer sacrifices to call on birds to help them. If the birds are willing to hear these prayers, they come in huge numbers and eat the locusts. But if someone captures one of these birds, he is punished with death according to their laws. If he is pardoned for taking the bird and is released, the other birds become very angry and will not return again if called.

The following story told by Artemidorus is very hard to believe.

There is a certain harbor on the sea coast called Two Crows. A pair of crows live there with right wings that are partly white. If two people have a disagreement about something, they come to the shore and each throws a cake of barley into the air. The birds will fly up and eat one cake but scatter the other. The one whose cake is scattered is judged winner in the dispute.

The Druids and Their Teachings

The druids, who have captured the imagination of many modern people with a spiritual inclination, were the priests and priestesses of the ancient Celts. They were also judges, scientists, physicians, and much more. There is so much we don't know about the ancient druids, but as the brief passages below reveal, what we do know is fascinating.

The druids study the ways of nature, but also the principles of morality and human behavior. The Gauls consider the druids the most just of people and trust them to judge both public and private disputes. In the past, they even stepped between Celtic armies at war and stopped battles. Murder cases are also judged by the druids. They believe that when condemned prisoners are sacrificed, the land will prosper.

The druids say that the human soul and the universe

as a whole are indestructible, but at some time in the future both fire and water will overcome the world.

It is said that the teachings of the druids began in Britain. Even today those young druids most diligent about their studies will travel to Britain to complete their training.

The druids, unlike all other Gauls, are exempt from serving in the army and from paying taxes. This is attractive to many young people and so they freely commit themselves to the long course of druidic study. Others are sent by their parents. In their druidic schools they learn an endless number of poetic verses, so many that it often takes them twenty years of training. They are not permitted to write down anything, for this weakens the memory.

The druids have many teachings that they hand down to those learning their ways, such as the secrets of the motion of the stars, the size of the cosmos and the earth, the order of the natural world, and the powers of the immortal gods.

Women of the Druids

Among the ancient Celts, women as well as men could be druids. In fact, of the handful of individual druids we know from classical times, most were the women mentioned in these three passages from imperial biographies dating to the latter centuries of the Roman Empire. They show that faith in the druidic power of prophecy continued long after the Roman conquest of Gaul.

The female druid exclaimed to the emperor as he left, "Go ahead, but don't hope for victory nor put any trust in your soldiers."

While the future emperor Diocletian was still a young soldier he was staying at a tavern in the land of the Tongri tribe in Gaul. Every day he paid his bill to the landlady, who was a druidess. One day she said to him, "Diocletian, you are both greedy and cheap!" He jokingly said back to her, "Don't worry, I'll be more generous when I'm the emperor." She responded, "Don't laugh, for you will indeed be emperor when you've killed the boar."

On certain occasions Aurelian would consult with druidesses from Gaul to discover whether his descendants would rule after him. They told him no name would be more famous than the line of Claudius. Indeed, our current emperor Constantius is of the line of Claudius.

Visions from the Dead

In many ancient cultures, people sought inspiration and wisdom from their ancestors who had passed from this life to the next. The Celts did this as well, according to a second-century BCE Greek poet named Nicander from the town of Colophon in Asia Minor, as recorded by the Christian author Tertullian several centuries later. This is the earliest reference we have to the Celtic belief in life after death.

It is often said that the dead truly live because we have visions of them in dreams. The Nasamones receive oracular inspiration from sleeping at the tombs of their dead parents, according to the writings of Heraclides—or maybe it was Nymphodorus or Herodotus. The Celts do the same, spending the night near the graves of their famous men, as Nicander confirms.

Reincarnation and Rebirth

In the Greek and Roman religious world, the dead—good and bad alike—were commonly believed to dwell in a gloomy after-life of dust and darkness. The Celts, however, were an exception to this common ancient view of life after death. Although we may associate reincarnation and rebirth of the soul with the ancient religions of India, the Celts also believed that the human soul survived death and was reborn in time into another body.

A teaching like that of Pythagoras is strong among the people of Gaul, that human souls are immortal and that after a certain number of years they pass into another body. Because of this belief, some of the Gauls will put letters to the dead in the fires of funeral pyres, so that those who have gone from this life may read them.

*   *   *

The most important teaching of the druids is that the soul does not perish at death, but passes from one body to another. Because they teach that death is merely a transition, they are able to encourage fearlessness in battle.

Divination and
Human Sacrifice

As much as it might make us uncomfortable, there is little doubt that the practice of human sacrifice was part of early Celtic religion. The evidence of written sources and archaeology is simply too strong to deny. But this should be tempered by the fact that human sacrifice was rare and also found elsewhere in the ancient world—even on occasion among the Romans who so protested against the practice by the Celts. Moreover, the era of the Greeks and Romans was a time of savage war, widespread infanticide, wholesale crucifixions, and the slaughter or enslavement of entire populations who found themselves on the losing side of a conflict. The occasional ritual killing of a condemned criminal by the druids should be seen in this wider context. We should also consider intriguing modern archaeological evidence that some victims of human sacrifice were high-status Celts or even druids themselves who went to their deaths willingly, to be, in their belief, reborn into a new life.

The druids predict the future through a strange and unbelievable method of divination for the most important matters. They carefully anoint a human victim, then stab him with a small knife above the diaphragm. When the man collapses from his wound, they interpret the future by how he falls, in which way his limbs convulse, and especially the patterns of his spurting blood. In this ritual, the druids place great trust in their ancient traditions of divination.

They will also keep a criminal under guard for five years, then impale him on a pole in honor of their gods. Later they will burn his body on an enormous pyre with the first fruits of harvest. At other times they will use prisoners of war in their sacrifices.

The Gauls are all a very religious people. Because of this, those who suffer from terrible diseases or face dangers in battle will hold a human sacrifice—or at least vow to do so. The druids are in charge on such occasions. They believe that unless one life is offered for another, the immortal gods will be offended. These sacrifices are done in both public and private settings. Some of the Gauls will build enormous wooden figures that they fill with human victims and set on fire, killing all of them in the flames. They believe that the sacrifice of thieves and other criminals is most pleasing to their gods, but when they run out of guilty persons they will sometimes sacrifice others.

In times not so long ago, the Gauls would also burn

faithful slaves and beloved friends at the climax of a grand funeral.

> *Cruel Teutates, pleased by human blood,*
> *horrid Esus with his barbaric altars,*
> *and Taranis, more cruel than Scythian Diana.*

Mistletoe, Sacred Plants, and Magical Snake Eggs

Aside from sacrifices, we know few details about the actual religious practices of the ancient druids. Almost all we do know is thanks to a curious though often skeptical Roman writer named Pliny who finished an encyclopedic natural history just before he perished in the volcanic eruption of Mount Vesuvius that destroyed Pompeii in 79 CE. His brief passages are a treasure house of varied information about the druids.

I must mention the admiration the druids have for the plant called mistletoe. The druids, who are the priests of the Gauls, hold nothing more sacred than this plant and the tree on which it grows, the oak (as if that were the only place it grows). The druids worship only in oak groves and won't perform any sacred rituals unless at least a branch of that tree is present. The druids even get their name from the Greek word for "oak," which is *drus*. They think that anything that grows on an oak is sacred and was sent by a god.

In fact, mistletoe doesn't really grow that well on oaks. But still the druids will go to great efforts to search it out on that tree and cut it off only on the sixth day of the Moon's cycle, because the Moon is then growing in size but not yet halfway through its course. They use the Moon to measure months and years, as well as their grand cycle of thirty years. In their own language they call mistletoe a name meaning "all-healing."

The druids hold their sacred meals and sacrifices under oak trees, leading forward two white bulls with horns bound for the first time. A priest dressed in white then climbs a tree and cuts down the mistletoe with a golden sickle so that it drops onto a white cloak. They then sacrifice the bulls and pray that the god will grant his gift to the one to whom he has given it.

They believe that a drink made from mistletoe will restore fertility to livestock and act as a remedy to all poisons.

There is a Gaulish plant called *selago* much like the Sabine herb savin. It must be picked without an iron tool while passing the right hand through the left sleeve, as if you were stealing it. The harvester—who must wear white and have clean, bare feet—must first offer a sacrifice of bread and wine. It is carried about on a new piece of cloth. The druids of Gaul say that selago should be used for warding off all dangers and that its smoke is good for eye diseases.

The druids also gather a marsh plant called *samolus,* which must be picked with the left hand while fasting. It is useful for cow diseases. The person who gathers it must not look backward or put it anywhere except in the watering trough of cattle.

There is a kind of egg famous in Gaul but not mentioned by Greek writers.

In the summer months a large number of snakes will roll themselves together into a ball held together by their own saliva and a secretion from their bodies. The druids say this mass of snakes produces an object like an egg that is called an *anguinum,* which the hissing snakes throw up into the air. They also say it must be caught in a cloak before it hits the ground. If you take their egg, you had better have a horse ready because the swift snakes will chase you until blocked by a stream. They say a genuine anguinum will float upstream even if covered in gold.

Like holy men from other lands, the druids say these eggs can only be gathered at some certain phase of the moon—as if anyone could make snakes and the moon work together.

I saw one of these eggs myself. It was small and round like an apple but with a hard surface full of indentations that looked like those on the arm of an octopus. The druids value them very highly. They say the eggs will help you to gain a favorable decision in a lawsuit or from a ruler. This is ridiculous as is plainly shown by a Gaulish man and Roman knight of the Vocontii tribe who kept one hidden under his cloak during a trial before the emperor Claudius. He was executed, as far as I can tell, for this reason alone.

The Holy Island
of Women

Women were honored among the Celts more than in most other ancient cultures. Though the roles of the sexes were not perfectly equal in Celtic societies, women could, on occasion, fight as warriors in battle and more frequently served their communities as bards and druids. The role of women in religious life seems particularly important among the Celts.

The Greek philosopher Posidonius recorded the story of a sacred island in southern Gaul inhabited only by women who were devoted to a religious practice that seemed very strange to him—but of course religious rituals often seem strange and are misunderstood by those viewing them from the outside, even by such a sympathetic foreigner as Posidonius. It may be that the violent ritual he records was a real occurrence among the women, but as with other stories he relates, it's also possible he is passing on an earlier myth about the women of the island. In any case, this is the earliest story we have of a community of women in Celtic religion, a theme that continues into Christian times.

Posidonius says that there is a small island in the Atlantic Ocean at the mouth of the Loire River on which only women from the Samnitae tribe live. These women are possessed by Dionysus and appease this god by mysterious ceremonies and sacred rituals.

No man ever comes to the island, but the women sail to the mainland to have sex with men and then return.

Each year the women take down the roof of their temple and build it again in a single day before it grows dark. Each woman carries a load of materials to add to the roof, but if one of them drops her load she is torn apart by the others. They then take the pieces of her body and carry them around the temple shouting with wild bacchanalian cries until their frenzy passes. But you should know that the woman who drops her load is always bumped by someone.

Two Gaulish
Magical Spells

We rely so much on the Greeks and Romans for our knowledge of ancient Celtic spirituality that it is most welcome and extraordinary for archaeologists to discover ancient tablets written by the Celts themselves. Both the following inscriptions from Gaul were written in the native Gaulish language on lead in the first century CE, more than a century after Julius Caesar conquered the land for Rome. They show not only that Celtic religion survived under the new rulers but it thrived as a spiritual path for different groups.

The first tablet was deposited in a sacred spring of water—a common portal to the underworld—near the modern town of Chamalières in south-central France and is by a group of men beseeching the gods for help. The second was found near Larzac in southern France and is a magical, perhaps darker, invocation by a group of women using family titles that suggest a religious sisterhood.

Some of the words in the tablets are unknown and many of the phrases are uncertain, but the supernatural power of these remarkable inscriptions still speaks to us clearly after two thousand years.

THE TABLET OF CHAMALIÈRES

I call on the divine Maponos Avernatis by means of this magical tablet.

Come to us who are named below, by the power of the underworld spirits:

> C. Lucios, Floros Nigrinos the invoker, Aemilios Paterinos, Claudios Legitumos, Caelios Pelignos, Marcios Victorinos, Asiaticos son of Atthedillos.

It is the oath of the Strong One they shall swear:

> The small will be great,
> the crooked will be straight,
> the blind will see.

THE TABLET OF LARZAC

Behold:

> a magical incantation of women,
> their special underworld names,
> the magical incantation of the seeress who weaves this prophecy.

The goddess Adsagsona renders Severa and Tertionicna enchanted and bound.

Below are written the names of those women who share in this prophetic curse and underworld magic:

Banona daughter of Flatucia, Paulla wife of Potitos, Aiia daughter of Adiega, Potitos father of Paulla, Severa daughter of Valens and wife of Paullos, Adiega mother of Aiia, Potita wife of Primos and daughter of Abesa.

The Sacred Isle

Cut off from the ordinary world, islands were holy among the Celts. They were places where people longing for spiritual growth would go to seek communion with the gods or later, the God of the Christians. Whether the majestic Tír na nÓg—the Irish land of eternal youth—or scattered rocks in the sea like Skellig Michael settled by Christian monks, islands were places of pilgrimage and magic.

The earliest surviving passage about Ireland in ancient records, stretching back perhaps five centuries before the beginning of the Christian era, is in fact a poem that speaks of the whole island of Ireland as a sacred place, an idea echoed by many people in the centuries to come.

From here it is a two-day voyage
to the Sacred Isle—for so the ancients called it—
a land rich in turf among the waves of the Ocean.
The Hierni live there, filling the land.

The Magical Islands
of Ireland

The twelfth-century Christian bishop Gerald of Wales collected many stories on his travels around Ireland. Some are undoubtedly true, others fanciful. His stories of supernatural islands in Irish lakes are placed in a Christian setting, but may well preserve traditions dating to before the Christian era. In any case, they show the vibrant spiritual world of medieval Ireland in which angels, demons, and astonishing miracles were never far from the lives and minds of ordinary people.

There is a lake in the northern part of Munster that has two islands, one large and one small. On the larger island there is a church that has been a holy site from ancient times. On the smaller island is a little chapel that is tended by a few celibates who are called Worshippers of Heaven.

Any woman or even a female animal that lands on the larger island dies immediately. This has been proven by those who have tested this story by bringing over female dogs, cats, or other animals that have all perished straightaway. Male birds nest on the island, but female birds avoid it by instinct as if it were infested with a plague.

On the smaller island no one ever dies, not in the past nor today. It is therefore called the Island of the Living. If an inhabitant of the island comes down with a fatal disease, they will live in misery and pain until they beg for death. Then they are brought over to the larger island and die as soon they are carried onto the shore.

There is an island on a lake in Ulster that is divided into two parts. On one side stands a beautiful and pleasant church of great holiness visited frequently by angels and saints. The other side of the island is craggy and possessed by demons who have been seen there performing their wicked rites.

The evil half of the island has nine pits. If anyone should spend the night in one of the pits—something that has been done by a few rash men—demons will seize and torture him all night long with fire and water. At the end of the night there will scarcely be a spark of life left in the poor soul. But it is said that whoever undergoes this torment will escape the punishments of hell, unless they commit some very serious sin.

Imbas Forosnai: The Ritual of Illuminating Knowledge

This ancient Irish ritual comes from a Christian source called Cormac's Glossary *by Cormac mac Cuilennáin, the ninth-century king and bishop of Cashel in southern Ireland. But the origins of the tradition, with its references to gods and its opposition by the Christian church, must lie deep in the Celtic past. It is similar to the invocation of supernatural* awen *("spirit, inspiration") in early Wales in the next passage. The* fili *("seer, poet") who performs this Irish ritual to gain knowledge is a poet and bard whose role stretches back to the world of the druids.*

IMBAS FOROSNAI—IT REVEALS TO THE FILI WHAT IS PLEASING AND WHAT NEEDS TO BE REVEALED

This is how it is done:

The fili *chews a piece of raw flesh from a pig or dog or cat.*
He puts the chewed flesh on a stone behind the door.
He chants over the flesh and offers it to false gods and summons them to him.
He continues this into the next day, chanting over the palms of both his hands.
He then summons idol gods to him so that his sleep may be undisturbed.
He puts the palms of his hands on his cheeks, then lies down to sleep.
People watch over him to make sure that no one interferes and that he is not disturbed.
Then the thing that he seeks is revealed to him.

This ritual can take up to three days—but it could take twice or three times that long, whatever length of time is needed.

It is called *imbas* because a palm (*bas*) is placed on this side and that side around (*im*) his face or head.

Patrick forbade this ritual and the *teinm laída* ("chewing the marrow"). He vowed there would be no place in heaven or on earth for someone who practiced them, for they are a denial of Christian baptism. *Díchetal di chennaib* ("an incantation from the ends"), however, was allowed as a part of the poet's art, for it springs from learning and no offering to demons is needed to accomplish it, simply a telling from the ends of the bones.

Awen: The Welsh Gift of Magical Inspiration

As in the previous passage from Ireland, the Celtic people of medieval Wales also preserved an ancient tradition of magical inspiration for their seers. Those chosen to receive this gift were called the awenyddion ("those possessed by awen")—a word of common Celtic origin with the Irish ái ("spirit, breath, wind"). In this Welsh ritual there is no chewing of animal flesh, but many of the other elements are similar to those of the Irish imbas forosnai, including visions in sleep or in a state of separation from the everyday world.

The twelfth-century churchman Gerald who records the experience of the awen-possessed was of an educated Welsh-Norman background, so he could be suspicious of the seemingly pagan ways of his countrymen (and most definitely of the Irish), though in this case he was willing to accept awen as a gift of the Christian God.

There is a certain group among the Welsh called the *awenyddion*—the inspired people—who act as if they are possessed by demons. They are found nowhere else.

If you consult them about any problem or question you have, they will go into a trance and lose control of their senses as if seized by some spirit. They will not answer your question in a coherent way, but evasively and with many riddles in what seems to be meaningless and disjointed words, though beautiful to hear. However, if you listen carefully you will find the answer you are seeking.

After this period of ecstasy, they can be roused as if from a deep sleep by a violent shaking and are brought back to their senses. They must be forced awake by others and will remember nothing of what they said earlier. If they are asked the same question a second or third time or by someone else, they will say something totally different.

It could be that ignorant and yet somehow inspired demons speak through them unaware in their frenzy. For the most part this gift is given to the *awenyddion* in their dreams. Some of them say it is as if honey or sweet milk is being poured onto their mouths, others that it seems like writings with words are pressed against their lips.

Before they go into such a trance, they invoke the true, living God and the Holy Trinity, then they pray their sins will not prevent them from revealing the truth to their listeners.

Because of similar events in ancient writings and the Christian scriptures, we should not be amazed that those who receive the inspiration of God as a gift of grace should sometimes seem to have lost their minds.

The Irish Story
of Creation

One of the most striking aspects of the history of Celtic spirituality are how easily the Celts were able to integrate Christianity into their own ancient beliefs. One Irish retelling of the biblical story of creation from The Book of Invasions *adapts and blends the stories of Genesis with Irish mythology.*

In the beginning God created the heavens and the earth.

But God himself has no beginning and no end.

The first thing God made was unformed matter and the light of the angels.

After the six days of creation, God rested, though he was not tired.

God gave the care of heaven to Lucifer, along with the nine orders of the angels of heaven. He gave the care of the earth to Adam and Eve, along with their children.

After this Lucifer led into rebellion a third of the angels. But God defeated him and imprisoned him in hell along with his angels.

Lucifer was jealous of Adam, thinking that the man would be raised up into heaven to take his place. And that is why he went out in the form of a serpent to tempt Adam and Eve. Adam was then driven from paradise into the lands of the earth and was fruitful.

After many years, Cesair the granddaughter of Noah came to Ireland with fifty women and three men just forty days before the great flood. Noah had said to her, "Arise and go to the western edge of the world, for perhaps the flood will not reach it."

But the flood came and they all perished.

The Reincarnations of Tuán Son of Cairell

The Celtic belief in reincarnation found in ancient druidic sources is echoed in stories from Ireland even in Christian times. One of the best is the tale of Tuán, an elderly monk who lived many lives both in human and animal form.

One day a Christian holy man named Finnia arrived in Ireland with his disciples and was refused hospitality by a wealthy landowner among the Ulaid. His followers were upset, but Finnia said to them, "Be at peace, for tomorrow a good man will come to us."

The next day an old monk came to them and invited them back to his hermitage in the forest. They sang psalms and celebrated mass there. When they were finished, Finnia asked him to tell the story of his life.

"Why would you want to hear about that?" said the old

monk. "I would rather we speak about the word of God and the Gospel of Christ."

"Nevertheless," said Finnia, "it is the will of God that you tell us the history of this island." For Finnia knew who he was.

The old man sighed and began.

"My name is Tuán son of Cairell—and I have lived many lives.

"I came to Ireland long ago, a thousand years after the great flood of Noah, when the land was empty of people. Our leader was Agnoman of the race of the Greeks. We were strong and proud, twenty-four couples of men and women. We settled the island and flourished, so that we in time numbered a thousand souls. Then a great plague struck the land and killed everyone except a single man. I was that man.

"I went mad in my loneliness and fled from mountaintop to mountaintop, fighting off the wolves that hunted me. After many years alone I became old and decrepit. I could no longer run. I hid myself away on cliffs and in caves. Other settlers came to the island and I watched them from my hiding places, but I wanted nothing to do with them. My hair and nails grew long. I was shriveled, naked, and miserable.

"One night I lay down to sleep in a cave and saw myself pass into the shape of a mighty stag, a leader of a herd of many deer. I ran like the wind and led my herd all around the island. I saw the race of Nemed come with his family, but the sea took many of them and the rest died here on the land.

"I grew old as a stag and could no longer run. Men and wolves hunted me. One night I went back to the cave and I remembered! I remembered how to pass into another shape.

"I became a strong young wild boar then. I was in good spirits and became leader of a herd of boars roaming the island. I saw as Sémión and his people came to settle the island. The Fir Bolg were his descendants. Then weakness and age came upon me again. I couldn't keep up with the herd and so at last went back to my cave. I remembered all the creatures I had ever been. I ate nothing for three days and had no strength left.

"At last I passed into the shape of a hawk and was happy. I would fly across all of Ireland and watch, learning all things. I saw as Beothecht came and conquered this island. From his people were born many races, including the tribes of the gods and un-gods—or so some say. Others claim they were in fact angels cast out of heaven with Lucifer.

"I saw the Sons of Míl come to this island and conquer the Tuatha Dé Danaan. I grew old again as a hawk and came to rest in a tree above a stream. I could barely fly anymore and was afraid of other birds.

"I stayed there and ate nothing until I fell into the stream and became a river salmon. That was marvelous for me and I was happy. I swam everywhere and was never caught by the nets of men or the claws of hawks, though their scars are on me still.

"I grew old and slow. It was then I was caught in a net by a man named Cairell who was king of this country.

He brought me back to his home and cooked me for his wife. She alone ate me. I passed into her womb and began to grow. I could hear everything said in the house and remember it all. Then I was born and named Tuán son of Cairell. I grew to be a young man in the household of my father, who did not know the true faith of Christ.

"One day I heard the words that holy Patrick preached to our people. I was baptized then and came to believe in the king of all creation."

And this is the story Tuán told to Finnia and his disciples.

The Coming of the Tuatha Dé Danaan

The ancient Celtic gods never died in the memory of the Irish even in Christian times, but were instead transformed in their stories into powerful beings of magic who had come to Ireland long ago and continued to dwell in the land, though usually hidden from sight. The most powerful of these were the Tuatha Dé Danaan, who ruled Ireland before the Sons of Míl arrived in the land.

The Irish loved to tell stories about the Tuatha Dé Danaan, one of their favorites being how they arrived on the island and conquered the tribes who lived there before them. In this story recorded by Christian monks, the Tuatha Dé Danaan are not quite gods, but supernatural beings of an earlier age. The origins of the story, however, lie deep in pre-Christian Celtic mythology, in a distant age when gods like the Olympians and Titans of Greek legend or the Aesir and Vanir of the Norse sagas battled each other to rule the world.

Many people came to Ireland in ancient times, but it was the Tuatha Dé Danaan who ruled over the land before the dawn of our age.

Some say they were angels cast out of heaven when Lucifer rebelled against God, others claim they were human beings who had lived in the northern islands of the world and studied magical arts until they were an awesome power. But no one knows for certain.

They came wrapped in black clouds and plunged the island into darkness for three days. They brought with them four awesome instruments of magic. The first was the stone of knowledge called the Lia Fáil that still stands on the Hill of Tara. It would cry out when a true king of Ireland stood on it. The second was the invincible spear of Lug. The third was the irresistible sword of their king, Nuadu. The last was the cauldron of the Dagda that never grew empty of food.

The Tuatha Dé Danaan demanded that the Fir Bolg, who ruled the land then, yield Ireland to them, but they bravely refused and met them in battle in the plain of Mag Tuired. Eochaid mac Eirc, king of the Fir Bolg, was slain along with most of his people.

Nuadu, the ruler of the Tuatha Dé Danaan, lost his hand in the battle and could no longer be their king—for a king must be without blemish. The assembly then met and gave the kingship to Bres, whose mother was Ériu of the Tuatha Dé Danaan, but whose father was Elatha, king of a mighty people across the waves known as the Formorians.

But Bres was a wicked and stingy king who cared nothing for his people. The knives of the Tuatha Dé Danaan were not greased at his feasts nor did their breath smell of ale. They began to starve, while the Formorian people of the father of Bres came and took over the island. Even the great warriors of the Tuatha Dé Danaan became their servants, so that Ogma carried their firewood and the Dagda was forced to build them a fortress.

Finally the Tuatha Dé Danaan rebelled and drove Bres and the Formorians from Ireland. They fled back to their homeland where Bres gathered his forces to take back the island.

The Tuatha Dé Danaan made Nuadu king again, for the smith Dian Cécht had made Nuadu a hand of silver that moved as if he had been born with it. Nuadu then gathered all the Tuatha Dé Danaan on the Hill of Tara for a feast to celebrate a new beginning for their people. The doorkeeper Camall mac Riagail stood guard at the gate with orders from Nuadu to turn away anyone who wasn't useful to them.

While Nuadu and his people were feasting, a handsome young man came to the gate.

"Who are you?" demanded Camall.

"My name is Lug," said the young man.

"What is your craft?" asked Camall. "For no one without a craft useful for us may enter the feasting hall of Tara."

"I am able to build great things," said Lug.

"We don't need you," replied Camall. "We already have a builder."

"I am a smith of iron"

"We already have a smith."

"I am a leader of warriors."

"We already have a leader."

"I am a bard."

"We already have bards."

"I am a physician who can heal any wound."

"We already have a fine physician."

"I am a weaver of magic."

"We already have sorcerers."

"Well then," said Lug, "does Nuadu have anyone who can do all these things together?"

Camall went to the king and told him about the young man at the gate.

"Let him enter," said Nuadu. "For no one like him has ever come to Tara before."

Lug entered the feasting hall of Tara and took the seat next to the king. Ogma was so angry at this brash young man that he took a giant stone that could only be moved by eighty oxen and threw it at Lug. But Lug caught it and threw it back at Ogma. Then Lug took a harp and began to play so beautifully for the people feasting there that they wept with sadness and joy.

When Nuadu saw all that Lug could do, he made him captain of his army and gave him power to wage the coming war against Bres and the Formorians. Nuadu summoned all the druids and sorcerers of the land to Tara and they pledged to fight for the Tuatha Dé Danaan king. The Mórrígan came as well, fearful goddess of battle and prophesy, to pledge her help in the great battle ahead.

At last the Tuatha Dé Danaan met the Formorians on the plain of Mag Tuired. It was as if the sea were crashing against soaring cliffs. Countless warriors on both sides fell there. Weapons rang out, spears flew through the air, and rivers of blood flowed across the plain.

The battle raged for three days and three nights. At last Lug fought his way through the Formorians to Balor of the Deadly Eye. His eyelid was so big that it took four men to lift it—but when they did all who looked at it lost the will to fight and were slain. Lug took a sling stone and blinded Balor.

Finally Lug captured Bres and was about to kill him when the former king pleaded for his life.

"Spare me and the cows of Ireland will always give milk," said Bres.

"Not good enough," answered Lug.

"Then spare me," pleaded Bres, "and I will teach you how to make the whole land of Ireland fertile forever."

Lug then agreed to spare his life.

And so the Tuatha Dé Danaan conquered the Fir Bolg and the Formorians, ruling the land from north to south, from the eastern to the western sea.

The Songs of Amairgen

Once the godlike Tuatha Dé Danaan had defeated their enemies and ruled over Ireland, they faced a new challenge from a Celtic people known as the Sons of Míl. These invaders sailed across the sea from Spain to claim Ireland for themselves. Although they were not gods like the Tuatha Dé Danaan, the Sons of Míl were fierce and determined warriors. Among them was a bard named Amairgen who knew how to use the magic of verse to fight against the Tuatha Dé Danaan. In two of the most enchanting poems in the Irish language, he called on the spiritual power of Ireland itself to help his people defeat the Tuatha Dé Danaan.

When the Tuatha Dé Danaan roused the waves of the sea against the invading Sons of Míl, the bard Amairgen stood on the bow of the lead ship and sang out:

> *I invoke the land of Ireland,*
> *rising from the mighty sea.*

Mighty are its highlands filled with meadows.
Filled with meadows are its rainy forests.
Rainy are the rivers overflowing with waterfalls.
Overflowing with waterfalls are the spreading lakes.
Spreading are the fountains of its people.
A fountain is its gathering of people,
the gathering of the people of the king of Tara.
Tara is a tower of the tribes,
the tribes are the Sons of Míl.
Warriors on their ships, their vessels.
Ireland itself is a mighty vessel.

And then the winds of the storm grew calm and the Sons of Míl reached the land of Ireland.

As he set his right foot upon the shore of Ireland, Amairgen recited this poem:

I am the deep wind on the sea.
I am a mighty wave upon the land.
I am the fearsome crashing of the sea.
I am a powerful stag who has fought seven combats.
I am a swift hawk on the cliff.
I am a pure tear-drop of the sun.
I am the most beautiful of flowers.
I am a valiant boar.
I am a swift salmon in a pool of water.
I am a vast lake on a plain.
I am the skill found in beautiful arts.
I am a spear that wages battle for glory.

I am a god who makes the tribes for kings.
Who can explain the stones of the mountains?
Who can evoke the ages of the moon?
Who can say where the sun sets in the west?

The Taking of the
Síd Mound

The following story tells of how the great síd *mound at New-grange changed ownership among gods—a tale told more than once in Irish stories—and features a favorite theme of the playful and fluid nature of time in Celtic mythology.*

There was once a wondrous king of the Tuatha Dé Danaan in Ireland named the Dagda ("good god"). His power was strong even after mortal men and women took the island from them. But the Tuatha Dé Danaan made sure the newcomers could produce little grain and milk until they made a treaty of peace with them.

It was the Dagda who distributed the *síd* mounds of Ireland to the Tuatha Dé Danaan—to Lug, Ogma, and all the rest. But he kept the best of *síd* mounds, the great tomb at Newgrange, for himself.

One day after every *síd* had all been distributed, Mac

Óc ("the son of youth") came to the Dagda and asked for a mound of his own to dwell in.

"I have nothing to give you," said the Dagda. "Every *síd* has been given away."

"In that case," said Mac Óc, "may I have your *síd* here for just a single day and night?"

And the Dagda agreed.

The next day the Dagda returned to his *síd* and said to Mac Óc, "It is time for you to leave my home. Your day and night have passed."

"But," said Mac Óc, "all of time is made up of a day and a night, over and over again. That is what you granted me. The *síd* is mine."

And the Dagda had to admit he was right. He left the *síd* mound at Newgrange, which for each day and night ever after belonged to Mac Óc.

The Adventures of Nera in the Otherworld

The Otherworld is one of the most fascinating aspects of Celtic spirituality—a supernatural world parallel and similar to our own, but utterly different. It is inhabited by gods and other divine or semidivine beings, but might be entered by humans at places such as grave mounds, caves, river crossings, or magical islands. The easiest time to cross into the Otherworld is during the Irish celebration of Samain (modern Halloween) when the boundary between our two worlds is the thinnest.

The early Irish story below of a young warrior named Nera has many aspects of Otherworld tales found elsewhere in Celtic literature, such as passing between worlds, supernatural beings, and time operating very differently from our own world. As Nera learns, to enter the Celtic Otherworld is to leave human limits and logic behind and surrender yourself to something both terrifying and wonderful.

On the cold, dark night of Samain at the beginning of winter, Ailill and Medb had gathered their followers together at their fortress of Cruachan. They had hanged two prisoners the day before and were feasting with their household.

Ailill then stood up and proclaimed, "Whosoever dares to go out into the night and tie a twig around the foot of one of the dead prisoners hanging on the gallows will receive a great reward from me."

But no one dared to leave the fortress on such a dread night, for spirits roamed the land.

Then a young warrior named Nera arose and said, "I will go claim that reward."

"Do so," said Ailill, "and I will give you a fine sword with a hilt of gold."

Nera armed himself and went out of the gate of the fortress to where the two prisoners were hanging. He took a supple twig and tried three times to tie it to the foot of one of the prisoners, but each time it came undone.

"You have to put a special spike into the twig or it won't stay," said one of the dead men.

And so Nera put a spike into the twig.

"Well done, Nera," said the dead man. "But please do me a favor. I was thirsty when they hanged me. Would you take me to one of the nearby houses to get a drink?"

Nera agreed and the dead man climbed onto his back.

They went to the first house, but the prisoner said, "Not here."

They went to the next house, but the prisoner said, "No, this is not the right place, either."

They went to the third house and Nera put the prisoner

down onto the ground. The dead man went into the house and found a tub of dirty water. He took a drink, then spat the water into the faces of those in the house so that they died.

After this Nera carried the dead man back and hanged him on the gallows.

Nera was almost back at the walls of Cruachan when he saw a troop of strange soldiers surrounding the fortress. The whole structure was ablaze, with the severed heads of Ailill, Medb, and all his friends piled in front of the gate.

The army began to march away and so Nera joined them in line. They went deep into the nearby cave of Cruachan.

"There is a man in our troop," said one of the soldiers. For they felt his presence.

"What shall we do with him?" asked another.

"Take him to the king," said a third.

And so Nera went before the king. It was warm and sunny in that land, a beautiful spring day filled with flowers and the songs of birds.

"Why are you here in our world?" asked the king.

"I followed your army," answered Nera.

The king sighed and said, "Leave me, Nera. Go to that house you see nearby. An unmarried woman lives there. Tell her I ordered her to care for you. Just bring me a bundle of firewood every day for sparing your life."

And so Nera did as the king commanded. As the days passed by, he brought a bundle of firewood every morning to the king. Every day as he left, he saw a blind man carrying a lame man on his back. They always went to a pond in front of the king's fortress, where the blind man would ask, "Is it still there?"

"Yes," the lame man would say.

When Nera got back to the house of the woman, he asked her what the men were doing.

"The king keeps his golden crown in that pond," said the woman. "Those two men have been ordered to keep watch and makes sure no one steals it. But since the king trusts no one, he blinded one man and the other he made lame so they couldn't take it from him."

"I don't understand this place at all," said Nera. "Why did the king burn down Cruachan and kill my friends?"

"So they wouldn't steal his crown," said the woman. "But what you saw is the future in your world, though the past in ours. Return to your world and you will find your friends still alive. Warn them that our king is coming to kill them. They should strike him first if they want to live."

"But no one will believe me," protested Nera.

"They will if you take them these spring flowers," she said, handing him a bouquet of wild garlic, primrose, and buttercups. "It is almost winter in your world, but it is spring in ours."

So Nera took the flowers.

"And by the way," said the woman, "I am pregnant with your child. If your people come here to destroy this place, send me a message first."

Nera agreed and made his way back through the cave to the cold and darkness of Cruachan. He found Ailill, Medb, and all his friends still sitting around the fire on the same Samain night. He told them what had happened and showed them the flowers, so that they believed him. Ailill, Medb, and their warriors gathered their weapons and prepared to march into the cave that very night.

Nera rushed back into the cave ahead of them. He found the woman there with a little boy. She embraced him with great joy, as if she hadn't seen him for a long time.

"I told the king you were very ill," said the woman, "and so I carried a bundle of firewood to him every day in your place."

She held the little boy in front of her.

"Nera, this is your son. Our cattle have also prospered here as well while you were gone and we now have a great herd."

"But my people are on their way to destroy this place!" said Nera. "What should we do?"

The warriors of Ailill and Medb descended into the cave and ravaged the fortress of the king, taking the golden crown with them back to Cruachan.

But Nera remained there with his family and cattle until the end of time.

The Lives of Étaín

Reincarnation and rebirth played an important role in Celtic spiritual beliefs in pre-Christian times and continued to capture the imagination of the Irish and Welsh people long after the arrival of the new faith in their lands. One of the best stories of multiple lives from medieval Celtic literature is an Irish tale of a woman named Étaín. Filled with supernatural events and otherworldly beings, it is above all a story of the enduring power of love.

The king of the Tuatha Dé Danaan was the Dagda, also known as Eochaid Ollathair, the Father of All. He was a powerful being who could bring storms from the heavens, rich harvests to the earth, and control time itself.

One day he fell in love with a woman named Eithne—but she was already the wife of Elcmar, who lived at that time in the great *síd* mound of Newgrange by the River Boyne. Eithne wanted to sleep with the Dagda as well, but her husband Elcmar was jealous and not easily deceived. The Dagda, however, came up with a plan that Eithne approved. He sent Elcmar on an errand, but made time stand still for him while away.

Meanwhile the Dagda went to Eithne and made love with her. She became pregnant right away and nine months later bore him a son who she named Óengus, the Young One, for she said, "Young is my son, conceived and born in a single day." She then gave him to the Dagda.

Elcmar returned from his journey thinking only a day had passed. He had no idea the Dagda had slept with his wife or that she now had a son by the king.

The Dagda took young Óengus to the house of his companion Midir to be fostered. The Dagda told Midir not to tell the lad who his real father was, but to keep the secret from him until it was time. Thereafter Midir raised the child as if he were his own son. He had three hundred foster sons and daughters, but Óengus was his favorite and a child of exceptional beauty.

One day Óengus got into a fight with one of the other boys in the house of Midir, Triath of the Fir Bolg, whose people had ruled Ireland before the coming of the Tuatha Dé Danaan.

"I shouldn't lower myself to speak to the son of a slave," Óengus said contemptuously to Triath.

"At least I have a father," Triath spat back at him. "You don't even know who your parents are."

Óengus went in tears to Midir and begged him to tell him who his father and mother were.

"Your father is Eochaid Ollathair, the Dagda, and your mother is Eithne, wife of Elcmar of the *síd* by the River

Boyne. I raised you so that Elcmar might not know your mother had been unfaithful to him."

"I will go to my father now," said Óengus, "and claim my inheritance."

Óengus went with Midir to Uisnech, in the center of Ireland, where the Dagda was holding an assembly of all the Tuatha Dé Danaan. Midir called the Dagda aside and said that Óengus wished to speak with him privately.

"Welcome, Óengus," said the Dagda. "What is it you want from me?"

"I want for you to acknowledge me as your son," replied Óengus, "and give me land of my own."

"I gladly claim you as my son," said the king, "but the land I would give you is already taken by your mother's husband, Elcmar. He holds the *síd* mound of Newgrange and will not give it up easily."

"But what shall we do for the boy?" asked Midir, for he loved Óengus.

"You yourself go to Newgrange on the day of Samain," said the Dagda, "a day of peace when no one will have weapons at hand. Elcmar will be standing on the *síd* with a forked stick of hazel and a golden brooch on his cloak. Threaten to kill him, but don't. Instead make him promise to give Óengus the rule of the Bruig na Bóinne for a single day and night. When Elcmar returns, tell him Óengus is now the owner of his *síd*—for all of time is made of a day and a night never ending."

Midir did as the Dagda said and tricked Elcmar into giving Newgrange to Óengus, who became ruler of the great *síd* of the River Boyne with all its land and people.

Óengus was grateful to Midir and wished to reward him for all the kindness he had shown. He gave him a fine chariot and a beautiful cloak, but that wasn't what Midir desired most.

"Grant me," said Midir, "the most beautiful woman in Ireland."

"She is not mine to give," said Óengus, "for that woman is Étaín, daughter of Ailill, a king in Ulster. But I will go myself and ask for his daughter as your wife."

And so Óengus went to Ailill and asked for his daughter Étaín.

"That will not happen," said Ailill, "unless you pay the price I demand."

"What price is that?"

"In exchange for Étaín, you must clear twelve forests in a single night so that I may graze my cattle there."

"It will be done," said Óengus.

Óengus knew he couldn't perform such a task alone, so he went to his father the Dagda, who gladly did it for him.

Óengus then returned to Ailill to claim Étaín.

"Not so fast," said Ailill. "You must change the course of twelve rivers in my land so that they flow clearly to the sea."

"It will be done," said Óengus.

And again he went to the Dagda, who changed the course of the rivers in a single night.

Óengus then returned to Ailill to claim Étaín.

"Not so fast," said Ailill. "You must finally give me the weight of my daughter in silver and gold."

"Bring her forth and weigh her," said Óengus.

And so they brought Étaín into the hall of her father.

She was radiant in her beauty beyond any woman in Ireland.

They then put her on a scale and weighed her. Óengus gave her father her weight in silver and gold, then took the girl back to Newgrange, where he gave her as a bride to Midir who was overcome with love for the girl and slept with her that night at the *síd* of Óengus.

When Midir left, Óengus embraced him and warned him to be careful.

"Midir," cautioned Óengus, "your first wife, Fuamnach, will not welcome this woman Étaín into your home. Fuamnach is a powerful druidess, daughter of the great druid Bresal, and she is full of magic."

Nonetheless, Midir brought the beautiful young Étaín to his home as his new wife and bade Fuamnach make her welcome.

At first, Fuamnach seemed to be full of kindness to the girl. But one day when Midir had gone away, the druidess took a branch of purple rowan and struck Étaín with it, so that the girl turned into a puddle of water on the floor by the hearth. Fuamnach then left Midir's house and went home to her foster father, Bresal.

The puddle of water that was once Étaín lay cold on the floor by the hearth fire. Then at last the heat of the fire, the warmth of the air, and the power of the earth transformed the water into a beautiful purple butterfly.

Midir returned home to find both his wives gone, but saw the butterfly and knew at once what had happened. He loved Étaín with all his heart, but he knew he didn't have the power to change her back into a woman.

The purple butterfly that was now Étaín followed Midir wherever he went. The sound of her humming wings was sweeter than the finest music of harp or pipe. Her fragrance was so wonderful it would drive away hunger from a starving man and the drops of dew that fell from her wings would cure any illness. Midir would fall asleep each night with Étaín humming beside his bed and she would wake him if any danger came near.

But Fuamnach was not finished with Étaín. She vowed that she would make the creature miserable wherever she might go. She stirred up a great wind and blew Étaín away from Midir. For seven years Étaín was unable to come to rest on a branch or tree.

At last Étaín was blown to Newgrange where Óengus ruled as king. There she landed exhausted in his lap. Óengus knew her at once and kept her as safe as he could, but it wasn't long before Fuamnach heard where she was and stirred up another great wind to drive her across the hills and rivers of Ireland.

Many centuries passed. At last the beautiful butterfly that was Étaín came to rest on a ceiling pole in the house of Étar, a great warrior of Ulster. The weary butterfly fell from the ceiling into a golden cup held by Étar's wife, so that the woman swallowed her unaware.

Étar's wife became pregnant and nine months later bore a girl. They did not know why, but she and Étar gave her the name Étaín and loved her very much.

Étaín grew and prospered in the house of Étar. One day she was washing herself in a river near the sea when she saw a horseman coming toward her across the plain.

He was very handsome with golden hair and was dressed in a fine green cloak with red embroidery.

There was something familiar about him, as if she had known him in another life. At last, he rode away.

Étaín grew into the most beautiful young woman in Ireland. In time Étar gave her to Eochaid, who was then king over the whole land. He slept with her and made her his wife. She tried to be happy, but she never forgot the man on the horse.

One day when Étaín was in the forest alone, the man came to her again.

"Who are you?" asked Étaín in wonder.

"I am Midir of Brí Léith," he replied. "I was your husband in another world, another time, a thousand years ago. But I still love you with all my heart."

And then Étaín began to remember.

"Please come away with me now, Étaín," Midir pleaded.

"I love you, but I cannot break faith with my husband Eochaid," she answered. "You must win me from him honorably."

"And so I shall," answered Midir.

The next day as Eochaid was sitting in his hall, a stranger to him entered and bade him greetings.

"Who are you?" asked Eochaid.

"I am Midir of Brí Léith," the man answered, "and I have come to play *fidchell* with you and win."

Eochaid laughed.

"I am the best *fidchell* player in the land, but you are welcome to try. If you win, I will give you whatever you wish."

Midir then played the king and won. Eochaid was angry but kept his word.

"What is it you wish?"

"I wish," said Midir, "to give your wife Étaín a kiss."

"A bold thing to ask a husband!" said Eochaid. "But let it be done."

The king's men brought Étaín into the hall and stood her before Midir. But Eochaid suspected a trick and placed his finest warriors in a circle around the room. There was no way to escape.

Midir came forward and gently kissed Étaín.

"You have had your kiss," declared Eochaid. "Now leave my kingdom and never return."

"As you wish, my lord," replied Midir, who wrapped Étaín in his arms before anyone could stop him and flew with her out of the smoke hole in the roof.

"Stop them!" shouted Eochaid, but it was too late.

Midir and Étaín lived together in happiness and love from that day forward—and there was no magic that could separate them ever again.

The Story of the Shannon River

In early Ireland, there was a tradition known as **dindshenchas,** *which told the origin of almost every river, mountain, and place on the island. Many of these stories involved divine figures and are often tragic, in as the following tale of the Tuatha Dé Danaan maiden Sinann (Shannon in English), the granddaughter of the Celtic sea god Lir, who gave her name to the greatest river of Ireland.*

How did the shining Shannon River get its name? I'll tell you now in language true.

The wild and gushing Well of Connla lay in the Otherworld beneath the blue waves of the sea. Seven streams flowed from it, but the greatest of these was the Shannon.

Nine hazel trees of Crimall the sage dropped their fruit into the well. They possessed awesome magic and were full of druidic power. Strange as it seems, the leaves and flowers of this tree sprouted at the same hour—and the fruit did as well! When these nuts were ripe, they would drop from the tree into the well below and sink to the bottom. Salmon would then come and eat them.

Listen! From the juice of the nuts came the magical bubbles of *imbas*—the magic of divine inspiration—drifting down the flowing rivers of Ireland.

There was a beautiful girl with golden hair, sprung from the Tuatha Dé Danaan, bright of eye she was and full of life, Sinaan, the daughter of Lodan Luchair Glan. This lovely young maiden had everything she could dream of—only the *imbas* was lacking.

She came one night to the river alone to see the glorious bubbles of *imbas* flowing down the stream. And found them she did, but all too eager she was. She leaped into the water to seize the bubbles for herself.

But alas, you cannot take that which is not meant for you. She drowned there that night, giving her name to the river forever.

Connla and the Woman of the Otherworld

Irish and Welsh stories of the Otherworld often involve someone meeting a supernatural being and falling in love. But encountering the Otherworld can involve terrible pain in leaving your old world behind.

Connla of the Red Hair was the son of Conn of the Hundred Battles. One day he and his father were with the druid Corann at Uisnech in the center of Ireland when Connla saw a beautiful woman in strange clothing coming toward them.

"Where have you come from?" Connla asked the woman.

"From the Land of the Living," she replied. "There is no death or sadness there, only joy and feasting."

"Who are you talking to, my son?" Conn asked him, for he could see no one else there with them, though he could hear a woman's voice.

"Come with me, Connla," said the woman, "to a land where you will never die. I have long watched you and I will love you forever if you will only follow me."

"Corann!" Conn shouted to the druid with them, "Cast a spell quickly and stop this evil spirit from stealing my beloved son away."

And so the druid cast a spell. But as she faded from his sight, the woman tossed an apple to Connla. For the next month, Connla wanted no food but the apple. But however much he ate, the apple grew no smaller.

After a month went by, Connla was walking arm in arm with his father by the sea when he saw the woman again, coming toward them in a crystal boat. His heart was filled with joy.

"Connla," said the beautiful woman of the Otherworld, "you live in a world of death and shadows, but the Land of the Living is waiting for you."

"Connla," his father pleaded with tears in his eyes, "do not listen to this woman. Think of your aged father. Please do not leave me. Don't let me die alone without my son."

"Father," said Connla as he wept, "I love you with all my heart, but I must go."

The woman led Connla to her crystal boat and cast off from the shore.

Conn could only watch in sorrow as his son sailed away from him forever.

The Boyhood Deeds
of Finn

The outlaw Finn mac Cumaill was the hero of many Irish sto-
ries from early times, with his tales surviving still in modern
folklore. The leader of a fían, a band of young warriors who
lived beyond the boundaries and rules of normal tribal life, he
was also famed as a poet and seer. The tales of his youth are
especially rich in magical inspiration and encounters with the
supernatural.

There was once a war between Cumall son of Trénmór
and the other clan leaders in Ireland. Cumall left his pregnant wife, Muirne, and went out to battle, but was slain by
the sons of Morna.

Muirne gave birth to a son she called Demne and gave
him over to be raised by two women who were both druidesses and warriors, Bodbmall and the Gray of Luachar,
for the sons of Morna sought to kill the infant. Bodbmall

and the Gray took young Demne into the deep forested mountains of Slieve Bloom and raised him in secret.

Six years later, Muirne set out to see her son and at last found the hut of Bodbmall and the Gray in the mountains. She saw Demne sleeping there and held him in her arms while she sang to him, but did not wake the boy. She charged the two guardians to raise him and train him as a hunter and warrior until the day came that he could bear arms.

While he was still a small boy, Demne went hunting by himself one day and found some ducks on a lake. He cast his spear at one of them and shaved the feathers off the bird, who promptly fainted. He then brought the duck back to the hut of Bodbmall and the Gray for supper.

Not long after, while Demne was still very young, he went out from the mountains and found a group of boys playing the game of hurley with sticks and a ball on the grass next to a fortress. They would not let him join them, but he fought them three times until he won and was allowed to play.

"Who is that boy?" asked a man on the walls of the fortress.

"His name is Demne," said the boys.

"You should have killed him," said the man.

"But we couldn't!" they cried. "He is too powerful."

"What is he like?" asked the man.

"He is fair (*finn*)," they replied.

And from that day forward Demne was known as Finn.

One day when Finn was crossing Slieve Bloom with his two guardians, they saw a herd of red deer on the hillside.

"It's a shame that we can't catch them," said the women.

"Oh, but I can," said Finn. He ran like the wind and caught two of the deer by the horns and dragged them back to the hut. From then on Finn did all the hunting for them.

When some years had gone by, Finn bade the two women farewell and went to learn the art of poetry from Finnéces the master bard. Finnéces lived beside the River Boyne where he had waited for seven years to catch a magical salmon at the Pool of Féc. It had been foretold to him that if he could eat the salmon he would gain great wisdom.

Finnéces at last caught the salmon and told Finn to cook it for him, for he was weary. After he woke, the boy brought the cooked fish to his master.

"Did you eat any of it, boy?" demanded Finnéces.

"No sir, but I burned my thumb on it while it was hot and put my thumb into my mouth to suck on."

Finnéces sighed, for he knew the magic and wisdom of the salmon had passed to Finn. After that, whenever Finn needed to know something, he would put his thumb into his mouth and chant the *teinm laída,* then it would be revealed to him.

Finn left Finnéces and traveled across Ireland to find Cethern son of Fintan, to learn more of poetry from him. Cethern taught him well, but then left with his companions to seek the hand of Éle, the most beautiful woman in Ireland, at the *síd* mound of Bri Éle, for she was of the Tuatha Dé Danaan. All the *síd* mounds of Ireland would open on the evening of Samain and that was when men would seek Éle to be their bride. But every Samain, Éle would refuse and one man seeking her hand would die.

Finn was angry that men died at the hands of the Tuatha Dé Danaan and was determined to end the killing. At the next Samain, he took his magical spear and hid himself between the hills of the Paps of Anu, each of which had a *síd* mound on top. As night fell, the veil between the two worlds fell away and Finn saw a man emerge from one of the mounds to go to the other. The man was carrying a live pig, a cooked calf, and a bundle of wild garlic.

Finn threw his spear at the man in vengeance for the deaths of those who had sought the hand of Éle and the man fell down dead. Then the women of the *síd* came forth and began to wail. He seized one of them and wouldn't release her until his spear was returned, which the people of the *síd* did.

And these are the boyhood deeds of Finn.

The Story of Gwion Bach and Taliesin

The Welsh shared in the ancient Celtic poetic tradition with the Irish and many of their earliest stories also tell of magical inspiration and otherworldly encounters. The story of young Gwion Bach—who becomes the great poet Taliesin—has much in common with both the boyhood story of Finn and the themes of rebirth found in the Irish tales of Tuán and Étaín, but with its own unique Welsh sense of spiritual power.

In the days when King Arthur ruled the land of Britain, there was a nobleman named Tegid Foel who was married to a sorceress and prophetess named Ceridwen. They had a son whose looks were so hideous that they called him Morfran, meaning "Great Crow." But his mother loved him very much and was sad when she saw it was terribly hard for him to make friends, so she sought to give him the spirit of prophecy.

Using all her magical arts, she gathered together special herbs on certain nights and placed them into a boiling cauldron to simmer for a year and a day. At the end of that time, there would be three potent drops that would give to whomever they touched the greatest of magical arts and the eternal spirit of inspiration.

Ceridwen hired a blind man to help tend the pot along with a small boy named Gwion Bach to guide him. For a year they stirred the cauldron until at last the day came that Ceridwen put her son Morfran next to the cauldron to catch the three drops when they sprang forth.

She was exhausted and asleep when the moment came and the three marvelous drops sprang out of the cauldron. But just as they were about to land on Morfran, young Gwion Bach pushed him out of the way so that the drops landed on him instead.

Ceridwen woke immediately and knew what had happened. She roared in anger and rushed from the house in pursuit of Gwion Bach—who had used his new powers to turn himself into the form of a hare. She transformed herself into a greyhound to chase him, then the two took on many other forms in turn as they raced across the land in different shapes with Ceridwen seeking to kill the boy.

At last Gwion Bach turned himself into a grain of wheat to hide in a barn, but Ceridwen changed into a black hen and ate him, swallowing him into her belly. She carried him there nine months until she gave birth to a baby boy. Her anger melted away when she saw him and she could not bring herself to do him any harm. So she placed the child into a small coracle and sent him out to sea.

Forty years later a good-hearted young nobleman named Elphin, who had little talent for success in the world, was fishing on the night of All Hallow's Eve. He was hoping to catch a salmon to eat when instead he found a small coracle in his net. He cut the net away and found a baby boy there with a shining forehead, and so called him *Taliesin* ("shining forehead"). Elphin lifted the baby from the little boat and was amazed as the boy began to sing:

> *Fair Elphin, do not weep.*
> *No catch you ever made*
> *was as good as the one tonight.*
> *I am small, but I am gifted.*

So Elphin took the baby home, after which he and his wife raised him with love.

One day in the nearby court of the local lord, there was a great gathering of the finest poets in the land. Elphin was foolish enough to brag that his own bard was the best, so that the lord cast Elphin into prison until he could prove his boast.

When he heard that his foster father had been imprisoned, young Taliesin went to the court of the lord and sat himself in a dark corner. As the great poets came in, the boy muttered a magic spell—*blerum, blerum*—as they walked by. When the poets rose and went before the throne to perform, all they could sing was *blerum, blerum*. The poets complained that an evil little boy in the corner had put a spell on them, so Taliesin was brought forward to face the lord.

"Who are you?" he asked the boy.
And the boy sang his answer:

I am the spirit of poetry
 and prophecy itself.
I was with God in the heavens
 when Lucifer fell.
I was in the ark with Noah
 when the flood came.
I move at will through the universe
 and will remain forever.
I was once called Gwion Bach
 but now am Taliesin.

After this he sang many things of what had been, and is, and what is yet to come. The lord then ordered Elphin to be set free and for Taliesin to be honored forever after by all the people of the land.

The Ancient Irish Horse Sacrifice

One of the strangest stories from early Ireland comes again from the twelfth-century Christian clergyman Gerald of Wales who traveled across the island and recorded his observations. He considered the Irish to be a barbaric and semipagan people, even if they had supposedly become Christians centuries before.

In this passage he writes of a ceremony that took place in the far northwest of the country when a new rí, or local king, rose to power in his tribe. The ritual has close parallels to the Ashvamedha sacrifice performed in ancient India in which a king would be confirmed as ruler. In both India and Ireland—at opposite ends of the common Indo-European cultural world—the horse was considered a unique symbol of royal sovereignty. In Ireland in particular, the horse was also a divine link uniting the king and the land itself, a common theme in Celtic religion and culture.

There are some things I am embarrassed to include in my account of Ireland, but my task as a historian demands that I mention these events, even if they might not be quite proper for my readers.

There is among the Kenelcunill in the northern and most distant part of Ulster a certain people who proclaim their king in a ritual that is altogether wicked and abominable. When the whole tribe is gathered together in a single place, a white mare is brought forward into the middle of them. The man who is to be inaugurated—not as a king but as a beast and outlaw!—has sexual intercourse with the animal in front of the whole crowd, claiming that he, too, is a beast. The mare is then immediately killed and cut up into pieces, which are cooked in a huge cauldron of boiling water. When this has cooled somewhat, the new king climbs into the cauldron and bathes himself in its waters. He sits there surrounded by all his people as they eat the meat of the horse that is brought to them. He himself dips his mouth into the broth in which he is bathing and drinks it, not using a cup or even his hands.

When this unholy ritual is finished, the man is declared king and sovereign over the land.

The Confession of
St. Patrick

Many legends have grown up around the man we know as St. Patrick such as battling druids, using the shamrock to explain the Christian Trinity, and driving the snakes out of Ireland (there never were any on the island). But the real story of his life is even more remarkable than the myths. Patrick was born into a wealthy family in the province of Britain at the end of the Roman Empire. He was raised as a Christian by a grandfather and father who were clergymen, but Patrick rejected his family's religion early in life and became an atheist. He was kidnapped by Irish pirates as a teenager and sold into brutal slavery in Ireland, but eventually escaped to Britain after a profound spiritual awakening. He then felt the call of God to return and preach the Christian gospel in Ireland, where he remained for the rest of his life.

We know his story because of the survival of copies of two letters he wrote later in his life. The first, presented here, is known as the Confession, but is really an autobiographical declaration of his beliefs and work in Ireland in the face of accusations from

British bishops. This deeply personal letter reveals a man who suffered great hardship in his life and at times was overcome with depression and despair, but nonetheless persevered against all odds to help bring a new faith to the Irish people.

My name is Patrick and I am a sinner. I am not a sophisticated man. I am the least worthy of all Christians and indeed despised by many.

My father was named Calpornius. He was a deacon of the church. His father was the priest Potitus. I come from the town of Bannaventa Berniae. My father owned a villa near the town and it was there I was kidnapped when I was about sixteen years old, along with many others. We deserved our fate because we—because I—had turned our backs on God. I was brought here to this island at the end of the earth.

But in Ireland the Lord increased my understanding so that I might turn from my sins and open my heart to him. He saw my misery and had mercy on me in my youthful ignorance. He comforted and protected me as a father would his own son.

Listen as I declare my faith:

There is no god but God. There never was and there never will be. He is uncreated and has no beginning or end. Indeed, in him all things have their beginning. He rules over all creation.

Jesus Christ is his son. He was present with God always and spiritually begotten before the beginning of this world, indeed before the beginning of anything. How this is possible we cannot know, but it is true. Through him all things were created, both those things we can see and those we cannot. He became a human being on this earth and died, but he conquered death and was taken back to heaven to be with God, who has given him all power on earth and under the earth. Every tongue will someday confess that Jesus Christ is Lord and God. He will judge both the living and the dead, rewarding each according to their deeds.

The Holy Spirit has been given to us abundantly by God and is the gift and promise of eternal life. He makes those who believe into children of God who will share in the inheritance with Christ.

This is the God we believe in—one God under the name of three, the Trinity.

Although I am far from perfect, I want my friends and family to know what kind of man I am, so that they might understand my heart.

I have long thought about writing this letter, but I hesitated until now because I am not an educated man. You can easily see from my Latin how limited my education is. I am ashamed that I can't write better and match proper words to my feelings—but still, I will not be silent.

In my youth I was foolish and ignorant, never looking to the future. But I was taught a powerful lesson in humility. I was like a rock stuck deep in the mud with no way out. But God in his mercy came along and plucked me out of the mire and placed me on top of a wall. Because of this I must proclaim that I am blessed and will give thanks to the Lord, now and forever.

When I was brought to Ireland as a slave, I tended sheep every day. I also learned at last to pray. My faith, my spirit, and my love for God grew every day, along with my respect for him. Sometimes I would pray a hundred times in a single day and a hundred times again at night, even when I was in the woods and mountains. I rose before the sun to pray in rain and cold and snow.

One night while I was sleeping, I heard a voice speaking to me, "You have fasted well. Soon you will go home." Later I heard the voice again, "Wake up! Your ship is ready."

But the ship was two hundred miles away in a place I had never been. Nonetheless, I ran away and left the man I had served as a slave for six years. I traveled with courage from God and wasn't afraid—until I came at last to the ship.

On the same day I arrived I asked the captain of the ship if I could sail with them, but he refused, saying there was no way he would let me on board. I didn't know what to do, so I went away a short distance and prayed. Then suddenly they shouted at me to come back to the ship.

"You can come with us," they said. "Make a pact of friendship with us however you wish." But I refused to suck their breasts. They were pagans, but I hoped they might come to believe in God, so I went on board and we set sail immediately.

We landed on a desolate coast three days later and then wandered about lost in an empty land for almost a month. We had no food and were starving.

The captain said to me, "Well, Christian, where is your

God now? You claim he is great and all-powerful, but your prayers don't seem to be working. We are dying in this wilderness and aren't likely to ever see anyone again."

But I said to them, "Turn your hearts to the Lord my God, for nothing is impossible to him. He will send food to us this very day."

And by the grace of God, that's exactly what happened. Suddenly a herd of pigs crossed the road in front of us. The sailors killed many of them and ate well for two days, even feeding their dogs all they wanted. They also found some wild honey and offered me some. But one of them said we have offered this up as a sacrifice to the gods, so I refused to eat it.

That very night while I was sleeping, Satan tempted me greatly. I will never forget it. I felt like a great rock had fallen on me so that I couldn't move my arms or legs. Somehow in my ignorance I managed to call on Elijah with all my strength. Then at that moment the rays of the sun reached me and took the weight off my limbs so that I could move. I think it was the power of Jesus Christ himself and the Holy Spirit helping me and crying out through me.

Not long after this, on the very night we ran out of food, we came at last to a settlement and were saved.

And so after years away, I came home to my parents at last. They welcomed me as a long-lost son and begged me never to leave them again after all we had been through.

I was there at home one night when I saw a vision of a man coming toward me. His name was Victoricus and he carried many letters with him. He gave me one and I began to read the title that said, "The Voice of the Irish." While I was reading it I thought I heard the voice of those who live by the woods of Voclut near the Western Sea crying out as if in a single voice, "Holy Boy, come back to us, we beg you. Walk among us again." I was pierced in my heart and could read no more. Then I woke up.

I thank God that he granted their prayer so that I went back to Ireland.

But years later, when I was accused by some of my church superiors of sins contrary to my role as a bishop, I was struck down mightily as if I would never rise again. They charged me with a sin I had committed more than thirty years earlier and had confessed before I was a deacon. It was something I had told a friend that I had done when I was maybe fifteen years old, before I even believed in God.

You all must understand, I didn't come to Ireland because I wanted to. Indeed I almost died here. But God used the experience to mold me into the person I am today, someone who works for the care and salvation of others. Before I was a Christian, I didn't even care about myself.

Many people here in Ireland have offered me gifts with weeping and tears. But I have refused to accept them. This has made some of my superiors in the church angry.

How is it that the Irish who have never known God, worshipping their idols and unclean things, have now become a people of the Lord? Even the sons of Irish kings have become monks and the daughters are becoming virgins of Christ.

There was one very beautiful young Irish woman of a noble family whom I baptized. She came to me a few days later and said that she wanted to become a virgin of Christ and so draw closer to God. Thanks be to God, that's exactly what she did. But the fathers of such women don't approve, so the young women are treated very badly and accused of terrible things. But still their numbers grow.

I don't know how many women believers have embraced the celibate life here in Ireland, not counting those who are widows and those who practice celibacy within marriage. But it's the slave women who suffer the most. They are subject to rape and terrible abuse. But even though they are forbidden to seek after a celibate life, the Lord gives them strength to go on.

I will not abandon these women to go back to Britain. God has ordered me to stay with these people the rest of my life. And so I will.

I have accepted nothing for my work among the Irish. Instead, I have spent all that I have. I have no wealth remaining nor do I want any. Every day I expect to be murdered, kidnapped, enslaved, or something worse. But I am not afraid, for I have placed myself in the hands of God.

The sun rises for us each day by God's command, but it will never rule nor will its brilliance last. Those who worship it will fall into terrible punishment. But we believe in and love the true sun, Jesus Christ, who will never perish.

And so I declare and testify the truth with joy in my heart before God and his holy angels that my only motive for returning to Ireland, from where I once escaped, was to preach the gospel and proclaim the promises of God.

I pray that any of you who believe in God and fear him—whoever you might be who read these words of the ignorant sinner Patrick—that none of you will give me any praise or credit for what I have done here in Ireland. You must believe that whatever I have done that was worthy, any small thing I accomplished, was the gift of God alone.

And this is my confession before I die. Amen.

St. Patrick's Letter to the Soldiers of Coroticus

Like his more humble Confession above, Patrick's Letter to the Soldiers of Coroticus was written in his later years in Ireland. But this shorter letter is filled with righteous anger against a British warlord named Coroticus who has kidnapped some and killed others of his Irish converts during a slave raid. Patrick is relentless in his condemnation of the supposedly Christian Coroticus and his men who would commit such violence against their own brothers and sisters in the faith.

My name is Patrick. I am a sinner and ignorant man—but I am a bishop in Ireland. I believe God himself appointed me to this position to serve as a stranger and exile among the Irish. He is my witness that what I say below is true.

I am not one to speak harshly, but my love of God and devotion to Christ have forced me to do so for the sake of my neighbors and children here in Ireland. For them I gave up my homeland, my family, and my very life. I live to teach those who do not know the love of God, even if some of you seem to despise me.

With my own hands I write these words to be delivered to the soldiers of Coroticus. I will not call them my fellow countrymen or blessed Romans, because their evil deeds have made them citizens of hell! They are bloodthirsty men who slaughter innocent Christians—the very ones I brought to life in God. These horrid men cut them down with their swords, even while my new Christians were still dressed in their white baptismal garments with anointing oil on their heads.

I sent a letter to the men of Coroticus the next day in the care of a young priest I had trained since he was a youth. I asked that they return the baptized captives along with some of the goods they had stolen from us. But they only laughed at my messenger.

I don't know who I should weep for more—the ones killed, the ones taken into slavery alive, or the men who took them, trapped as they are in the snares of Satan. Along with Satan and his demons they will certainly suffer eternal punishment in hell.

Let everyone know—all of you who fear God—that these men are strangers to God. They are murderers of fathers and brothers, ravaging wolves who devour their fellow Christians like bread. I earnestly implore you, my dear Christian brothers and sisters, do not seek favor from such men. Do not eat or drink with them. Do not take money from them until they repent and release the servants of

God and baptized handmaids of Christ, the ones he was crucified and died for.

As for those children of God so bitterly cut down by the sword, what can I say? I mourn for you—but I also rejoice. I can see you even now as you begin your journey to that place where there is no night, no sorrow, no death.

As for Coroticus and his evil band of murderers, what lies in store for them? They have distributed baptized Christian women like prizes, all for the sake of this world that will soon vanish like a cloud blown away by the wind.

I earnestly implore everyone who loves God to carry copies of this letter to all they meet. Read it aloud to anyone who will listen—even to Coroticus himself. May God inspire him and his men to come to their senses before it's too late so that they may free the captives they stole away. If they do, they might yet earn the right to be saved and live with God, both now and in eternity.

May the peace of the Father, Son, and Holy Spirit be with you all. Amen.

The First Synod of St. Patrick

A synod in early Christianity was a gathering of bishops to discuss issues facing their churches and to make rules for their members. Although the following instructions are traditionally attributed to St. Patrick, along with his fellow bishops Auxilius and Iserninus, they probably date to not long after his lifetime. The selection below from this synod gives us a fascinating glimpse into the internal problems of the Irish church at this early period and the sometimes tense relations between those who followed the ways of the old druidic religion and the members of the new faith.

1. Christians should not attempt to ransom captives on their own without permission of the church authorities. If they do, they should be removed from the church.

4. Those who have been given permission to collect money for a worthy cause shall not collect more than is needed.

6. If a priest wanders about naked without a tunic or doesn't cover his belly or doesn't cut his hair in the approved Roman way or if his wife goes about without covering her head, he shall be shunned by his congregation and removed from the church.

7. Any member of the clergy who arrives late to morning or evening prayers shall be removed from the church—unless he is a slave and not master of his own time.

8. If a member of the clergy gives a loan in any amount to a pagan and the pagan doesn't pay him back—as often happens—the clergyman must take the loss from his own resources, not those of the church. If a Christian priest resorts to single combat with a pagan, he shall be removed from the church.

9. Monks and nuns from different monasteries shall not travel together in the same vehicle nor stay in the same guesthouse nor even have long conversations with each other.

13. Alms from pagans shall not be accepted by the church.

14. A Christian who has committed murder or fornication or sworn an oath before a druid like the pagans, shall spend a year in penance for each offense.

16. Any Christian who believes there is such a thing as a *lamia* in this world—that is, a female vampire—

and accuses someone of being one shall be removed from the church for slandering a woman in such a terrible way. He or she will not be welcomed back into the church until he has recanted and done public penance.

17. A virgin nun who has renounced sex and then gets married shall be removed from the church until she repents and sends the man away.

19. A woman who has been married in the church and then leaves her husband shall be separated from the Christian community.

31. If one clergyman has a disagreement with another clergyman and hires someone to kill him, he shall be removed from the church and considered a stranger by all righteous people.

The Irish Penitentials

The penitential literature of the early Irish church strikes many modern readers as grimly harsh with its listing of sins and penalties, but it was actually just the opposite. In a spiritual world in which demonic forces were terrifyingly real and the fires of hell weighed heavily on the minds of Christians, the penitentials provided a remedy for the illness of sin and an assured hope that all would be well in the end. It is no coincidence that Irish Christians were among the first to fully develop the idea of pastoral handbooks for the forgiveness of sins since druidic law had long advocated the idea of enech *or face-price in which every crime against a person had a penalty that could be paid, usually in cattle, sparing the clan and community from an endless cycle of revenge and bloodshed.*

Anyone who boasts of his own good deeds shall humble himself. Otherwise his goodness means nothing.

Anyone who criticizes another with pride and contempt in his heart shall first make things right with the one he has offended, then he shall go and confess to a priest.

Anyone who reports a shameful sin about his brother without first talking with the brother in private shall make things right with him and then do penance for three days.

Anyone who in a joking way says something to hurt someone he loves shall do penance in silence for one or two days.

Whoever compels anyone to become drunk for the sake of fellowship and fun shall do penance as if he had become drunk himself.

Whoever commits theft shall do penance for a whole year. If he does it again, two years. But if the offender is only a boy, then thirty or forty days, according to his age and ability to understand his actions.

Any clergyman who has an excess of worldly goods shall give them to the poor. If he doesn't, he shall be excommunicated.

Anyone who cheats someone shall make restitution by giving back more than he has taken.

If someone has lied in ignorance, he shall confess his lie to the one he has deceived and to a priest. He shall then be silent for an hour. But if he has lied on purpose, then he shall be silent for three days.

If a monk loves a woman but has committed no sin beyond a conversation, then he shall do penance for forty days. If he has kissed and embraced a woman, one year in forty-day periods. If he has sinned only in his mind, then seven days is enough.

A layman who has sex with his neighbor's wife or virgin daughter shall do penance for a whole year on bread and water alone. And he is not allowed to be with his own wife during this time.

If a man has sex with his female slave, he shall sell her and do penance for a year. If he gets her pregnant, he shall set her free.

Anyone who hates another person shall live on bread and water until he leaves his hatred behind.

Whoever injures another man with a blow shall pay the man's medical expenses and do his work until he is healed.

Anyone who commits murder with hatred in his heart shall give up his weapons for the rest of his life.

Lazy people shall be given extra work as punishment.

Anyone who accidentally loses the eucharistic host—the sacred bread of communion and body of Christ—so that birds or animals eat it, he shall do penance for three periods of forty days each. If he did it on purpose, then for a whole year.

Whoever makes his friend sad shall make things right with him, whether he was justified or not.

Whoever carries a heavy weight of bitterness in his heart shall be healed by a joyful face and a glad heart.

The Legends of
St. Patrick

It seems that Patrick was largely forgotten by the Irish for two centuries after his death, but in the seventh century he was rediscovered and became the subject of many popular fables. Little remains in these wonderfully entertaining stories of the humble and very human Patrick we know from his letters. At the hands of writers such as the churchman Muirchú, Patrick becomes a mighty slayer of druids and worker of fantastic miracles.

In the days of holy Patrick, Ireland was ruled by a fierce pagan king named Loígure who reigned over all of the land from his fortress on the Hill of Tara. This wicked king surrounded himself with druids, soothsayers, sorcerers, and all those skilled in the arts of evil. The greatest of these were the druids Lothroch and Lucet Máel. This devious pair frequently warned the king that a new and foreign way of life would soon arrive on the island, bringing strange and dangerous teachings. They warned that the people of Ireland would be seduced and the old gods would be destroyed unless the new faith was crushed. They chanted this song of prophecy:

A man with a shaved head will come
with a stick bent on top.
He will sing evil songs
from his house with a hole in its roof.
From a table at the front of his house
all his family will sing in response:
"Let it be so, let it be so."

It was then that Patrick came to Ireland. His first wish was to ransom himself honestly from slavery from the master he had fled, a man named Miliucc. Patrick was determined to pay him twice the price Miliucc had paid for him. But when Miliucc heard that his former slave was on his way to him, he decided he would not accept the new faith and not allow his mere servant to have authority over him. He gathered all his goods together in his home and set fire to it with himself inside. Patrick arrived in time to see the flames and stood silently weeping at the sight.

Now the feast of Easter was drawing near and Patrick discussed with his companions where they might celebrate the resurrection of the Lord. Patrick decided on the wide plain of Brega near Tara, the center of heathenism and idolatry on the island.

They came to a hill near Tara and kindled the Easter fire there to proclaim their faith. But there was a law among the pagan Irish that no man could light a fire on that night ahead of the king. When Loígure saw the flames rising from the nearby hill, he declared that whoever had kindled it would be put to death. He himself with his druids and warriors went to the hill in war chariots.

Patrick met the king there in peace, but Lothroch, the king's druid, began to mock his faith. Patrick at once prayed to God so that the druid rose up into the air and then fell down on a rock, splitting open his skull and dying. The pagans were all very much afraid. The king threw himself down at the feet of Patrick, though he did not believe in the true faith and still planned to kill the holy man.

Patrick knew what the king intended, so he blessed his companions and they all turned into deer. Then they escaped into the forest.

The next day the king was feasting at his hall on the Hill of Tara when Patrick and his men suddenly appeared in the midst of them. The king was shocked, but bade the holy man to dine with them.

The druid Lucet Máel poured Patrick a cup of wine, but secretly put a drop of poison into the drink. Patrick, however, knew the druid was trying to kill him. He blessed the cup so that the wine froze like ice, then turned it upside down so that the liquid drop of poison fell out. He righted the cup and blessed it again so that the wine turned back into liquid.

After dinner, the druid demanded a contest of miracles there on the plain before Tara. He called snow down so that it fell on the plain up to the depth of a man's belt.

Patrick said, "We have seen what you can do. Now remove the snow."

"I do not have that power," said Lucet Máel.

"You can work evil but not good," said the holy man, then he made the snow disappear.

Next the druid invoked demons so that darkness fell across the land. But Patrick prayed and brought the sun out again.

Finally the druid said he would submit himself to be judged by fire. He demanded that Patrick send one of his men with him into a hut and set it ablaze to see which of them would survive. Patrick chose his young follower Benignus. The druid gave Benignus his own robe and took Patrick's for himself, thinking the robe held powerful magic. Then they both went into the hut and it was set on fire. After a short time there was nothing left but ashes, Patrick's robe, and the boy Benignus unharmed.

King Loígure then came to Patrick and accepted baptism, along with his people.

Patrick worked many miracles among the Irish from that day forth. And when the time came at last for the holy man to die, angels came from heaven and kept watch over his body, which smelled as sweet as honey.

The Goddesses Brigid

Brigid was a famous female saint of Ireland who lived in the genera-tion after St. Patrick, but the story of a divine woman named Brigid reaches much further back into Celtic history and mythology. There was an important goddess named Brigid ("the exalted one") long worshipped in Ireland, Britain, and elsewhere in the ancient Celtic world. Her special day of celebration was February 1, the holiday at the beginning of spring known in Irish as Imbolg—*which, by no coincidence, became the feast day of the Christian St. Brigid.*

The antiquarian glossary compiled by the medieval Irish bishop and king Cormac is our best source on the goddess—or rather the goddesses—Brigid. For as was often the case in Celtic religion, she was part of a divine trinity.

Brigid—a poetess and daughter of the Dagda. This Brigid was a female sage and woman of wisdom beloved by poets for her protection and care. That is why she is called the god-dess of poets. Her sisters were Brigid the physician and Brigid the smith. All these goddesses of Ireland were called Brigid.

The Life of St. Brigid

We sadly know very little about the historical St. Brigid. Unlike St. Patrick, she wrote nothing herself that has survived. All we have are stories written down over a century after her death. These are in the tradition of hagiographical wonder tales found throughout Europe in the early Middle Ages, though Brigid's have a particular emphasis on mastery over nature and kindness to women. In these stories we can glimpse a very real person of remarkable gifts and kindness who fought to make a better world for women in a religious and secular culture that was dominated by men.

Holy Brigid was born in Ireland of noble Christian parents and came from the tribe of Echtech. Her father's name was Dubthach and her mother was Broicsech. From the earliest days of her childhood she desired to do good.

It would be impossible for me to tell all of the amazing things she did, even in her youth, so I will relate only a few of the many miracles she performed in her lifetime.

When Brigid was still a young girl, her mother sent her to churn milk into butter with other girls her age. Brigid was compassionate and sought to please God, so she gave away the butter she had made to the poor and homeless. When at the end of the day it was time to give the butter to her mother, she was very afraid. But God, who is our helper in time of need, restored the butter that Brigid had given away so that she had more to give to her mother than any of the other girls. Everyone there saw this and marveled at the great faith that lived in the heart of this girl.

Not long after this, Brigid was inspired by God to seek a chaste life dedicated to God. Even though her parents objected, she went to a most holy bishop named Mac Caille and asked to be received as a virgin of Christ. He agreed and placed a white veil on her blessed head. She then fell to her knees at the altar of the church and offered thanks to almighty God, touching the wood at the base of the altar. Because of her purity, the wood is still green today and cures pilgrims who come to touch the altar.

One day when Brigid was cooking bacon in a cauldron for visitors, she felt sorry for a hungry dog who was begging at her side. She gave him some of the bacon, but when the meal was taken from the cauldron and given to the guests, there was no less bacon than if the dog had been given none at all.

There was another day when Brigid was working with harvesters in the fields and rain threatened to ruin their work. Although rain fell in torrents everywhere on the island that day, Brigid's fields remained dry from sunrise to sunset by the power of God.

Once when Brigid was tending sheep and grazing them in a grassy field, a fierce rainstorm fell down on her in the gathering darkness so that she was soaked to the skin. As the bright sun came out again, she went into the door of a darkened house nearby where there was a single, narrow ray of sunlight shining into the room. Thinking the beam of light was solid, she took off her clothes and hung them on the ray of sunshine. When the people in the house saw this, they were amazed and gave glory to God.

One other day when Brigid was tending sheep, a wicked but clever young man came to her in the field seven times in different disguises to ask her each time for a sheep so that he might have food for his family. Each time she gave him one sheep. But at the end of the day when she drove the flock back into the fold, there were no fewer sheep than when the day had begun. The thief, who had been watching this, came to her and confessed his sin and returned the sheep to her. But when she counted the flock again in his presence, there were the same number of sheep as at the beginning.

There was another time when a group of lepers came to Brigid seeking beer, but she sadly had none to give. There was though a bath full of water nearby, so she blessed it and turned the water into the finest beer and gave it to the lepers to drink.

Among Brigid's followers, there was a certain young nun who had taken a vow of chastity. But because of human weakness she had given into youthful desire and become pregnant, her womb swelling for all to see. Brigid, drawing on her matchless faith, laid her hands on her belly and blessed the young woman, so that the fetus inside of her disappeared without pain or childbirth. Thus the young woman became a virgin again and afterward did penance. For as scripture says, all things are possible for those who believe in God.

One day a woman from beyond Brigid's community went to the holy woman with her twelve-year-old daughter. The girl had been mute from birth and could not speak. The woman came before Brigid and bowed to her in reverence and received a kiss of peace. The girl then came forward and Brigid took her hands in her own. She asked the girl if she would like to take the veil and become a virgin of Christ when she grew older, not knowing she was mute. The mother told Brigid that her daughter was not able to speak, but Brigid smiled and said she would not let go of the girl's hands until she answered. When Brigid asked the girl again, she spoke aloud and said she wanted for her life what Brigid wanted. From that day forward her mouth was open and the young woman was able to speak.

There were many poor and sick people who came to holy Brigid from all over Ireland, drawn by stories of her kindness and miracles. One of these was an angry and bitter man in great pain from leprosy who rudely demanded that Brigid give him the best cow in her herd along with the best calf. She did not refuse him, but gave him the finest cow along with the best calf, though the calf was from a different mother. She had such sympathy for the sick man that she even gave him her own cart for his long journey home so that he would not be forced to walk. No calf would willingly leave its mother, but Brigid blessed this calf and placed it in the cart beside the man so that it would go with him. The cow she had given licked the calf as if it were her own and gladly followed the cart and calf across the land to the home of the leper.

After this some wicked thieves came from across a large river in another province on a cattle raid and stole some of Brigid's cattle. But on their return journey, the river became a towering wall of water and drowned the thieves. The cattle though were unharmed and returned to Brigid's fields.

Once there was a single wild boar of the forest who fled unexpectedly into a herd of pigs that was being tended by Brigid. The beast was terrified and dangerous, but Brigid spoke to him and blessed him so that he became peaceful and unafraid.

There was a kindly man who once came to Brigid from a farm several days away to ask that she send men to his farm to bring her some fat pigs as a gift, for he could not bring them by himself. Brigid agreed and sent a few of her people with him to his farm. After they had traveled only a day, they saw in the distance the man's pigs coming toward them. But they were not driven by men. Instead wild wolves of the deep forest had brought the pigs to them unharmed because of their reverence for holy Brigid. When the pigs arrived at the place of Brigid's men, the wolves left the animals there with them and returned to the woods.

I cannot forget to tell one of the most wondrous stories of blessed Brigid. There was once a foolish man who was walking around the fortress of a local king when he saw a fox. Thinking he was doing good for the king, he killed the fox in the sight of all. But the fox was in fact a beloved pet of the king and trained to do many tricks. The people hauled him immediately before the king, who said the man would be executed and his wife and children made slaves unless he could give him another fox who could perform tricks as well as the first. Blessed Brigid heard of this and was filled with pity. She set out for the king's fortress, praying all the way that God might grant her a way to save the man and his family. The Lord heard her prayer and sent a wild fox to her that she hid under her cloak. When she was standing before the king, she pulled out the fox and had him perform tricks even better than the one that had been killed. The king was overjoyed at his new pet and ordered the condemned man to be set free. Brigid then set off again toward home, but the fox she had brought to the king ran away from the fortress between the legs of the people there and returned to his home in the forest.

One day Brigid saw some wild ducks flying through the air above her. She called to them and they came to her. She embraced them and spoke to them kindly for some time before sending them on their way.

Once Brigid was working among the poor and needy near her church when she saw nine men in outlandish clothing marching by. They were part of an evil sect that worshipped demons and practiced the shedding of innocent blood. The men were shouting loudly and screaming. They had made a vow that they would not rest from their madness until they had committed murder and slaughter. Brigid ran to them and spoke many soothing words of kindness and peace so that they might realize their terrible sin, but they laughed at her and swore they would fulfill their vow. After they left Brigid, they came upon a young man alone and decided to kill him. They stabbed him with their spears and cut off his head, then danced around covered in blood. But when they at last grew calm, they saw there was in fact no blood on their weapons nor head on their spear. Brigid had created a phantom in their minds to satisfy their desire for slaughter. When the men realized this, they were deeply ashamed and came to Brigid begging her forgiveness and prayers. She received the men with joy and they turned their hearts to God from that day forward.

There was once a man named Lugaid who lived near the church of Brigid. He was the biggest and strongest man in the whole province and could lift as much as twelve men all by himself. But he had such a tremendous appetite that he feared he would starve his wife and children by eating all their food as well as his. He came to Brigid and begged her to help him. She prayed for him and from that day forward he ate no more than any other man, though his strength was undiminished.

I must also tell of the time Brigid went on a journey and stopped at the home of an old friend to spend the night. The woman she stayed with was poor and had very little to give, but she cared for Brigid as if she were receiving Christ himself. The woman had no firewood and only a single cow and calf, so she broke apart her loom and roasted the calf over its wood so that she might have something to feed her guest. In the morning Brigid embraced and blessed her, then left to go on her way. The woman returned to her small hut and found inside a new loom. She heard lowing and went outside, only to discover her cow had a new calf. The woman fell to her knees and praised God for the kindness Brigid had shown her.

Of the many remarkable works of holy Brigid, there is another I must record. Once there was a wicked man of noble birth who burned with lust for a beautiful young woman who wanted nothing to do with him. He schemed how he might have sex with her and decided to entrust to her a valuable silver brooch for safekeeping. He then secretly stole it back from her and threw it into the sea. Soon after this he came and demanded the brooch back from her safekeeping, but she said that she did not have it. He then said he would soon return and take her away as his slave to use her as he wished according to his most disgraceful desires. The young woman fled to Brigid in tears, not knowing what to do. Brigid listened to her, but before she had finished speaking a man came in with a fish for Brigid that he had caught in a nearby river. She cut the fish open to remove the entrails and found inside the silver brooch. The young woman then went to the assembly of the tribe and before everyone gave the brooch back to the wicked man, who confessed his sin to Brigid and all the people there.

These are just a few of the many wonders performed by holy Brigid in her life. No one can number the crowds who still come today to her church at Kildare bearing gifts on February 1, honoring the day she fell asleep in the Lord and was called to the heavenly mansions of the lamb of God.

The Holy Fire of St. Brigid

There were many wondrous stories told of Brigid after her death. In one recorded centuries later by Gerald of Wales, a sacred fire was reportedly attended by Brigid's female followers and, at times, by the saint herself. Like the divine hearth fire tended by the Vestal Virgins in the Forum of ancient Rome, this flame was the heart of the community and a connection to the divine power that guided them. And as with the Vestal Virgins, the care of the fire was a holy duty allowed to women alone.

Kildare in Leinster was made famous by blessed Brigid, who performed and still performs many miracles there. One of the most amazing of them is told in the story of the fire of Brigid.

It is said that the fire cannot be extinguished—or at least it never goes out because the nuns and holy women of the place feed it and care for it always. In all the centuries since the virgin saint died until now it has burned continuously. And even though an enormous amount of wood has been used in feeding the fire all these years, the ash pile has never grown.

In the days when Brigid was alive there were twenty nuns in Kildare tending the fire, including Brigid. After her death the number was never increased above nineteen. Each of these women takes turns caring for and guarding the fire, one staying beside it each night. When the beginning of the twentieth night comes, the nineteenth nun puts a pile of logs beside the fire and says, "Brigid, this is your night. The fire is in your care."

And so the fire is left alone. But in the morning the wood is gone and the fire still burns bright.

The Life of St. Darerca

Darerca, also known as Moninna, was, like St. Brigid, a virgin and abbess in the second generation of Irish Christians. The story of her life draws on earlier stories of women saints, especially Brigid, but with her own unique struggles and triumphs. Darerca was always seeking to find a place in Ireland for herself and the women who followed her in a culture and church dominated by men.

There was once a virgin named Darerca, also known as Moninna, descended from the tribe of the Conaille. Her father was a good man named Mocteus. She was born in Mag Coba and fostered as a child with a loving couple.

Darerca decided from an early age that with the help of God she wished to be a holy virgin for as long as she might live. While she was still young, St. Patrick arrived in her tribal lands to preach. Many came forward to be baptized in the holy water of Patrick and confirmed in the new faith by the touch of his hands. Darerca was small, but she pushed her way forward through the crowd to Patrick and presented herself before him. Moved by the Holy Spirit, Patrick saw her devotion and knew that God had chosen her to serve his people. He brought her to a pool called Bríu—which means "generosity"—and baptized her there.

Patrick instructed her in the faith and confirmed her as a holy virgin for Christ. He commissioned her to find and care for other virgins and so that they could encourage each other. He then left her in the care of a devout priest who lived near her parents. But she spent little time with this man. Because of her natural intelligence and tenacity, she was able to learn quickly all the priest had to teach her.

Darerca had meanwhile gathered eight virgins into her group along with one widow who had a small son named Luger. Darerca made the child her own foster son and after many years of instruction and training, appointed him as a bishop.

Once Darerca had learned all she could from the priest in her homeland, she set out into the wild roads of Ireland with her fellow virgins and other women followers, trusting in God. She came at last to the western islands where she found St. Ibar. She placed herself and her women under the holy man's authority and learned much from him.

Afterward, when Ibar left the western islands, Darerca and her companions went with him to the southern coast of Ireland, where he died.

Darerca then heard of an especially holy woman

named Brigid who lived at her own monastery in Kildare in Leinster. Darerca went to visit her, but accepted no honors from Brigid, always approaching her in great humility.

After this she left Kildare along with her followers and went to form her own monastic community. But there was a drought in Ireland at the time so that the springs and wells of the land ceased to flow. The followers of Darerca came to her and begged that she ask God for help, lest they all die. Darerca began to pray, but before she was finished a spring burst forth from the ground with so much fresh water that not only did her sisters have enough for their monastery, but all the surrounding farms could be watered as well.

Darerca possessed the spirit of prophecy, so that one day when a young girl came to her monastery saying she wanted to follow God as a holy virgin, Darerca told her sisters that the newcomer would bring only trouble to them in time to come. And indeed, after the girl had become a young woman, she was so inflamed by jealousy and hatred of Darerca that she brought nothing but misery to the monastery. But instead of expelling the young woman from the community, blessed and kind Darerca gave her the monastery for herself and left with her own faithful followers, taking only the clothes on their backs, trusting that God would provide for them.

And God did provide. Darerca went north and founded a new monastery with fifty of her women followers. Once she had settled the women there, Darerca went alone to visit her family, who had become Christians. Still, the land of the nearby tribe had in ancient times been a place of great magic.

Darerca stayed there by herself in the woods for a long time. It is said she didn't want to even look at a man. If she needed to leave her monastic cell, she did so at night. If she needed to go out in the day to visit sick women or ransom some girl from slavery, she would cover her face with a thick veil.

One night the blessed Darerca in her travels came upon a small group of virgins of Christ and stayed with them. The women had enough food for themselves and their guest, but they had nothing to drink but water. Darerca drew a jar of water from the well and blessed it. Then she poured into the cups of the women the finest wine they had ever tasted.

From there she went even farther into the wilderness to a distant mountain and gathered together there 150 women to live a life of holiness far from the ways of men. One night while she was there, she heard the sweet sounds of music and a large number of voices in the darkness. She was filled with fear, but went forth to a nearby holy mountain and found it was her own wedding feast being celebrated, with her own spouse, Christ the Lord.

When the time came at last for holy Darerca to pass from this world, angels were seen by her bed ministering unto her. She blessed her women followers and told them not to be sad, for she was going to be with the one she loved most of all. And then she died in peace and joy, surrounded by her virgins and taken into the heavens to be with Christ forever.

St. Columba and the Loch Ness Monster

Columba, known in Irish as Colm Cille ("dove of the church"),
was born into a royal family in northwest Ireland in 521, but he
rejected the privileges of nobility to become a simple monk in self-
imposed exile from his home in Ireland. He founded the monas-
tery of Iona on an island off the western coast of Scotland, which
soon became a center of Christian influence in both Ireland and
northern Britain. His life and miracles were recorded in the next
century by Adomnán, another abbot at Iona. In this story—the
earliest tale we have of the Loch Ness monster—Columba shows
the power saints were believed to have over the monsters and
dark forces of nature that threatened Christians.

On one occasion blessed Columba was traveling through
the land of the Picts when he came to the River Ness.
When he reached the bank, he saw some of the local people on the opposite shore burying a man who had just been

killed by a monster while he was swimming in the river. His companions had come to him in a boat but were too late to save him, though they were able to pull his body from the water with a hook.

Columba shouted across the river and asked them to send a man across to him with the towing cable moored to the opposite shore. Without hesitation a young man named Lugne took off all his clothes except his tunic and jumped into the water with the rope tied around him.

But the fearful monster deep in the river felt the water disturbed by the man swimming above him. The creature was still thirsting for blood and so burst through the surface of the water and began to rush toward Lugne with his mouth wide open.

The men on the opposite shore were terrified, as the monster was almost upon Lugne, but holy Columba raised his hand and invoked the name of God against the creature saying:

"Stop! You shall go no farther. Return to the place from which you came."

At the voice of the holy man, the monster was terrified and fled with all speed back to the depths of the river.

All the men present gave thanks for this wonder and to see their friend Lugne returned safely to them. Even those who were pagans were forced to acknowledge this awesome miracle and gave thanks to the God of the Christians.

Christian Irish Poetry

Early Irish Christian poetry is filled with beauty and spiritual imagery, as well as a keen appreciation of nature and often a subtle humor. The following are just two of the many poems composed in the centuries after St. Patrick.

Pangur Bán
(A Scholarly Monk and His Cat)

White Pangur and I
each pursues his special art.
His mind is set on hunting mice,
mine on my own work.

I love most of all, better than fame, to be quiet
with my book before me, seeking knowledge.
White Pangur isn't jealous of me.
He has his own playful work to do.

When we two are alone,
we never grow tired together,
each applying his own skill,
an endless game for both.

Oh, there are many times in battle,
a mouse will be caught in his net.
As for me, into my net
falls a passage of a book I at last understand.

Pangur directs his eye
against a hole in the wall.
Though my eyes are weak,
I direct them to learn sharp wisdom.

He is joyful in swift movement
when he catches his prey in his paw.
I too am joyful
when I understand a difficult, lovely problem.

We each do our own work
and don't bother the other.
We each follow our craft,
rejoicing in what we do.

Pangur is the master
of his daily work.
I perform my own work,
striving to understand what is difficult.

A Scribe in the Woods

A hedge of trees surround me,
a blackbird sings in my ears,
I cannot help but praise God.

Above the lines of my book, the birds sing to me.
The clear-voiced cuckoo, wearing his gray cloak,
sings to me from the tops of the bushes.

May the Lord save me from judgment,
but I cannot help but write
under the green branches of the woods.

The Voyage of Bran

To the ancient inhabitants of the Mediterranean lands, Ireland was a distant island on the far edge of the world. The Irish themselves felt that there was something liminal to their home, like a gateway to the unknown. From the earliest times the Irish people were great sailors and voyagers, but what lay to the west across the stormy waves of the Atlantic was a mystery that gave rise to many fantastic tales told in whispers by the hearth fires at night. The brief "Voyage of Bran" is one of the best of these, with strange islands, otherworldly women, gods of the sea, and time itself flowing in peculiar ways.

One day Bran, son of Febal, was walking alone by the sea near his fortress when he heard music behind him. Wherever he turned the music still came from his back. It was of such unworldly sweetness that he soon fell asleep. When he awoke, he saw next to him a branch made of silver with white blossoms. He took the branch in his hand and went into his house. His followers were gathered there looking at the wondrous branch when a woman in strange garments suddenly appeared in their midst and began to sing:

> *There is a distant isle*
> *around it the sea horses play,*
> *a fair land in the surging white waves.*
> *A delight to the eyes.*
> *An ancient tree is there*
> *and splendors of every color.*
> *There is no grief or sadness there,*
> *no tears, no treachery, no death.*
> *Bran, listen to me, come to us,*
> *and let go of your sorrow.*

And then the branch sprang from Bran's hand into the hand of the woman and she disappeared.

Bran was determined to follow her at once and find her island, no matter the dangers that lay ahead. He took with him three companies of nine companions, the best of his men, and set out in a coracle upon the sea.

They had been sailing west for three days when Bran saw a man in a chariot coming toward him over the waves. When he drew near, he greeted Bran and said he was Manannan, son of Lir, the god of the sea, and began to sing:

> *Bran sails across the clear sea*
> *and deems it a wonder,*
> *but I see a field of flowers*

on which my chariot rides.
You're not far now,
but much lies ahead.
Sea horses shine in the summer sun,
rivers pour forth a stream of honey
in the land blessed
by Manannan son of Lir.
You're not far now
from the island
where only fair women dwell.

The man in the chariot then left Bran and flew over the waves of the sea.

It wasn't long after that Bran saw a small island. He rowed about it while people there came to the shore and began to laugh. They would not speak to him, but only laugh with happiness. Bran at last sent one of his men to the shore, but that man himself burst into laughter right away. Bran left that place and called it the Isle of Joy.

Not long after this they came to the island where there were only women. The woman who had appeared in Bran's land was the leader of them. She came to the sea and called out from the shore, "Bran, son of Febal, welcome is your coming!"

Bran was afraid to go onshore, but the woman threw a ball of thread to him, holding one end in her hand. The ball stuck to Bran's hand and could not be removed. And so the woman pulled the coracle toward her from the sea.

Bran and his men followed the women into a large house where they were made welcome. Food was placed before them in dishes that were always full. When they were tired, they were led to a room with three times nine beds, one for each of Bran's men and a woman of the island to share, while Bran went with the leader of the women to her chambers.

It seemed to Bran and his company that they were there for only a year—but indeed it was much longer. Nothing was lacking for them and they were happy. But one day the spell was broken when one of the men, Nechtan, son of Collbran, was seized with a powerful longing for home. He begged Bran and his friends that they should sail back to Ireland. But the women of the island pleaded with them in tears not to go, saying it would be their death to touch their home again. But the desire to return to their land was too strong and they would not listen to the wise words of the women.

Bran and his men loaded their coracle and set sail from the island. Across the sea they sailed until at last they saw the cliffs of Ireland in the distance. They rowed to the shore where Bran shouted to some men gathered there, "I am Bran, son of Febal." But one of the men on shore laughed and said, "You cannot be him. He is the one in our ancient tales who sailed away across the sea centuries ago."

Bran's companion Nechtan could wait no longer. He leaped from the coracle and swam to shore. But as soon as he touched the sand of the beach, he turned to dust, as if he had been dead for ages.

Bran and his men had watched in horror what had

happened to their friend. They knew then that the women were right and they could never go home.

And so, as the men on the shore watched, the coracle with Bran and his companions sailed away into the sea and was never seen again.

The Voyage of St. Brendan

Like the previous "The Voyage of Bran," the journey of St. Brendan across the unknown sea is part of an ancient Irish literary tradition—but with a Christian twist. There are still magical islands and strange characters the holy man and his monks meet along the way, but there are also eccentric hermits, angels in exile, and one notorious sinner. "The Voyage of St. Brendan" is a wonderfully entertaining tale of a sea voyage across the Atlantic, but it is more importantly a metaphor for the spiritual journey of the Christian life.

Holy Brendan, son of Findlug, was born in the province of Munster. He was famous for his austerity, great miracles, and as the spiritual father of almost three thousand monks.

One day while he was serving the Lord, there arrived at his monastery a fellow priest named Barrind. The visitor fell on the ground before Brendan and wept, staying at his feet until his tears turned to prayers.

"Father Barrind," said Brendan to him kindly, "please rise and tell us what is troubling you."

So Barrind rose and began to speak.

"Father Brendan, one of my spiritual children named Mernóc left with a few monks to seek a life of spiritual solitude in the north. I heard that beyond the cliffs of Sleive League, he found a place of refuge and prayer called the Delightful Island. I sought to visit him there and set out in a boat. After three days I found his island. With Mernóc there were monks scattered about and living alone in caves, but coming together in faith, hope, and love to worship God. They live only on roots, fruit, nuts, and other greens.

"Mernóc walked with me to the far side of the island where there was a small coracle on the beach. He then urged me to come into the boat with him and sail to another island farther to the west called the Land Promised to the Saints, a place that will be the home for all of us someday at the end of this age of sorrow.

"We sailed toward the setting sun for only an hour, but suddenly a fog came upon us so thick we could scarcely see the front or back of the boat. Then at last a light came out and shone all around us. We landed on the shore of a wide and beautiful island. All the plants had flowers there and all the trees bore fruit. The very stones of the ground were delightful gems. We walked around the island for fifteen days before we found a great river. There a man appeared before us shining in a great light who said we could not pass beyond the river in this life. He also told us that there was no need for eating or drinking or sleep there and that the Lord himself was the light of that place.

"We left the angel by the river and returned to our boat. We boarded and sailed through the fog back to the Delightful Island, where Mernóc's monks welcomed us, marveling at the light in our eyes and the unworldly fragrance of our clothing. I stayed with them there two weeks without needed food or drink, then came here to tell you, Father Brendan."

Brendan praised God for the wondrous tale told by Barrind, but he was troubled about what to do. He took fourteen of his dearest brothers aside and shut himself into the oratory with them to seek their advice.

"My brothers," he pleaded, "help me to know the will of God. For it is my wish to go in search of the Land Promised to the Saints. But I cannot go alone into the unknown. Will you come with me?"

"Father Brendan," they replied as with one voice, "we have left our families, laid aside our earthly inheritance, and given our very bodies into your hands. How can you doubt us? Whether it means life or death, we are prepared to go with you with joy in our hearts."

Brendan gave thanks to God, then set out with his brothers to the end of a mountain that stretched far out into the sea, at the place now called Brendan's Seat. There was a small bay there with room for only one boat. Brendan and his men began to build a large coracle with a wooden frame and covered with the hides of oxen tanned in oak and smeared with fat. They brought with them extra fat and hides in the boat, along with provisions for forty days. In the center of the boat was a mast with a sail. At last when all was ready, Brendan and his brothers entered into the boat.

But just as they were about to set sail, three monks from Brendan's own monastery who had not labored to build the craft came and begged to go with them on their voyage. Brendan accepted them, but warned them that while one would find his reward, the other two would be gravely punished for the sins they held in their hearts.

Then they all embarked and steered westward toward the setting of the summer sun.

There was a favorable wind for fifteen days, but it ceased and they took to the oars. They became weary and despaired, for they were lost in the endless waves of the sea.

But Brendan said, "Do not fear, my brothers. God himself is our guide. Bring in the oars and spread the sail. He will do as he wishes with his servants and their ship."

They did as Brendan said, but nothing happened and the boat did not move. Then at last in the evening when the sun was setting, a wind began to blow. From where it came they could not tell.

For forty days the wind blew them swiftly across the sea. When their food and water were almost gone, they saw in the distance an island with cliffs rising into the sky. When they drew near they could find no place to land, but filled their water bags from streams that fell from the cliffs. For three days they circled the island looking for a place where they might come to shore, but found nothing.

Then at last when their strength was almost gone, they came to a small inlet and landed there. They stumbled onto the shore and fell down, praising God.

Then they heard a dog bark.

"God has sent us a messenger," said Brendan to the brothers. "Follow him."

And so they followed the dog inland to a large home. When they entered, they found a great hall furnished with chairs and beds, along with water to wash their feet. There was a table nearby with a fish and a loaf of bread for each of them. On the walls hung beautiful bridles and horns for hunting, all covered with the purest silver.

When supper was over and they had worshipped God, Brendan said to them:

"Go and rest, but be on your guard and take nothing from this place."

The brothers went to their beds and fell asleep. But Brendan, who remained awake, saw a demon in the form of a small child talking with one of the monks who had come late to the boat. Brendan then fell to his knees and prayed throughout the rest of the night.

When dawn came and the brothers gathered to leave the island, Brendan called them together and said that one of them had given in to the devil and become a thief. He pointed to the brother he had seen talking with the demon. The man fell to his knees and wept, pulling from his cloak a silver bridle.

"I have sinned," he said. "Please, Father Brendan, pray for my soul and forgive me."

Brendan stood before the man and said to the demon, "Come out of him, now!"

And immediately a small child leaped from the bosom of the man, crying and wailing to Brendan.

"Don't make me leave my home! I have lived here seven years. He belongs to me!"

"Get out!" shouted Brendan, "and torment no one else until the Day of Judgment."

With that the demon fled. Brendan turned to the man on the ground and raised him up.

"Take the body and blood of our Lord," said Brendan. "For here you will die and be buried."

And so the man took the Eucharist and fell down dead. Brendan and the brothers saw his soul rise up to heaven, but his body they buried there in the earth.

They all went sadly to the shore and found by their boat a young man carrying a basket of bread and a jar of water.

"Take this." he said. "You have a long voyage ahead, but neither bread nor water will fail you from now till Easter."

The young man then bade them farewell as they sailed from the island into the sea.

After some days passed, they saw another island and came near it, pulling the boat ashore on the beach. They found there flowing streams of clear water, full of fish, and many sheep, all white. Brendan told them to take one spotless lamb from the flock in preparation for the Easter feast. After they took the lamb, a man appeared among them with a basket of warm bread. He placed this before Brendan and fell on the ground at his feet.

"How is it," the man asked, "that in these holy days of Easter I deserve for you to eat the bread I have made with my own hands?"

Brendan lifted him from the ground and blessed him.

"Father Brendan," the man said, "God has ordained that you spend Holy Saturday here, but tomorrow you must go to that nearby island to celebrate Easter Sunday. Afterward you must sail farther still, to the Paradise of Birds."

So Brendan and his men spent the night there with the man, then set out for the nearby island. Their boat reached it and they pulled up onto the shore, but Brendan remained on board. The low island was rough and stony, without grass, with pieces of driftwood scattered about. Brendan celebrated mass there as he sat in the boat, but when he had finished the men began to kindle a fire onshore to roast the lamb they had brought from the other island. When they had built a fire, however, the island began to move like the waves on the sea. The men all screamed and were terrified, except for Brendan who knew what was happening. Abandoning everything, the brothers jumped into the boat and rowed away as fast as they could, watching as the island moved away and finally dive beneath the sea.

"My sons," counseled Brendan with a smile, "do not be afraid. That was not in fact an island but a fish, the greatest that lives in all the oceans. His name is Jasconius."

They sailed on until they came to an island with groves

of trees, grass, and blooming with flowers of spring. They landed at the mouth of a river flowing with pure and sparkling water. They followed it to the source at a spring covered by the largest tree any of them had ever seen. Perched in the branches were white birds that covered its branches.

Brendan sat down by the spring and watched the birds until one flew down. Its wings sounded like the softest tinkling of bells.

"If you are a messenger from God," said Brendan to the bird, "then speak to me and tell me why you are here on this island."

The bird looked at him kindly and then spoke:

"We were angels once at the time of the great rebellion when Lucifer and his followers were cast out of heaven. We did not side with them, but neither did we stand with God. The Lord sent us here as punishment, but we endure no sufferings, for God is just."

"Tell me," said Brendan, "what lies ahead for my brothers and me?"

"You," said the bird, "have endured one year on your voyage, but six years remain to you. After that you will find what you seek, the Land Promised to the Saints."

With that the bird rejoined its fellow angels in the tree and began to sing the most beautiful psalms that Brendan had ever heard.

For three months after that Brendan and his brothers were driven in their little boat across the waves of the sea. They could see nothing but water and his men soon despaired. But at last they came to an island and found a place to land. Waiting for them on the shore was an ancient monk with hair as white as snow and a face shining with light. He said nothing, but embraced Brendan and led them all silently to his nearby monastery—for they had taken a vow of silence so that they might listen more closely to God.

The abbot brought forth the monks of the place who welcomed them all with joy but no words, then fed them and led them to the church to worship God with them, singing hymns to the Lord.

Brendan and his men sorrowfully left the island to continue their journey, for it was not their place to remain there. They sailed on for days until they came to another island where they saw three choirs of men singing psalms to God on the shore.

Brendan turned to the second of the two brothers who had come late to the boat.

"Go onto the shore, my son, for the Lord has granted that you shall remain here with these monks."

Brendan embraced the man and sent him to the shore, where he joined the choir and sang as Brendan and his brothers sailed away.

They came next to an island where there were trees bearing fruit like grapes, but as big as apples.

"This is the meal the Lord has sent you," said Brendan to his men. "Take and eat."

They ate the fruit happily on the island for forty days, for they were sorely in need of nourishment and rest. The breeze smelled like pomegranates there and the wells were full of sweet water.

At last Brendan roused them, for they could not stay

and eat the fruit forever. They sailed on over the waves until they came to what seemed to be a mountain of pure crystal rising from the sea. It was so high they could not see the top and so smooth they could not climb the sides.

Then a fierce wind began to blow so that they were carried to the north for eight days. They came at last near a rough and barren island with no trees or grass. The dark land was covered with forges worked by a race of giant smiths whose hammer blows Brendan and his men could hear from afar. It looked to them as if the whole island were ablaze.

"We must get away from this place quickly," said Brendan. And so his men began to row with all their might, but the wind blew them ever closer to shore.

An enormous man on the island saw them and raised a shout. His neighbors all came down to the water with hot, glowing iron and threw the metal pieces toward the boat so that the sea boiled where the iron landed. At last the wind turned and the monks rowed away exhausted, still hearing the shouts of the giants and smelling the stench of the island behind them.

"We are at the very gates of Hell," said Brendan when they had moved far from the island of smiths. "Be on guard and pray that God might deliver his servants."

Soon they came to another island with a high mountain that was smoking and spewing flames from its top. The wind drew them close to the shore in spite of their rowing. The sands of the shore were black and the walls of the mountain looked like coal.

The last of the three brothers who had come late to the

boat rose up suddenly against his will and jumped out of the boat.

"Father Brendan," the poor man shouted, "I have not the power to resist. Have mercy and save me!"

But Brendan shook his head and wept, "Alas my son, I cannot. The Lord himself has chosen this as punishment for your sins."

Brendan and the brothers in the boat could only watch in horror as the man was snatched by a band of demons and carried away into the heart of the fiery mountain. Then in sadness they sailed away.

The wind blew the boat for seven days until at last they came to nothing more than a large rock in the sea. On the rock was a man sitting naked and enduring the crashing of the waves against him.

Brendan in amazement asked who he was and why he was being punished so.

"I am not being punished," the man replied. "This is my respite on holy days of the year. The remainder of the time I burn like a lump of molten lead in the fiery mountain of demons where your brother was taken. I am the greatest of sinners, the man who betrayed our Lord. I am Judas Iscariot."

Brendan spoke to him kindly and conversed with him there until demons came to take him back to the mountain.

"Go away, man of God!" they shouted. "We cannot come near until you withdraw."

"I will not leave this man until morning," said Brendan. "The Lord Jesus Christ has granted that he remain here with me till then."

"How can you protect him?" they demanded. "He betrayed your Lord!"

"Still, in the name of that Lord I order you to withdraw and leave him in peace till morning."

The demons gnashed their teeth and screamed in frustration, but yielded to the man of God and did not touch Judas until the sun rose. Then Brendan and his men sailed away.

One day near the end of their journey, the boat came to a small island. Brendan told his men to wait while he went ashore. He found there a man covered entirely with hair as white as snow down to his feet. The man radiated holiness, so that Brendan fell on his face before him. But the old man raised him up so that they might talk.

"How did you come here?" Brendan asked.

"My name is Paul the Hermit," the old man replied, "and I have been here since the days of holy Patrick long ago. I was at my monastery in Ireland when the spirit of Patrick himself came to me after his death and told me to go to a boat and let it take me wherever God might lead. The spirit of the Lord brought me here where I have lived without food for sixty years, nourished only by the water that gushes forth from this rock. And here I will die."

With the blessing of the old man, Brendan sailed away.

He and his men then came at last to a thick bank of fog where they could not see even the front or the back of their boat. Then the fog parted and they came to the shore of an island full of trees. They departed from their boat and walked about the island for forty days in endless light until they came to a great river. A young man appeared to them there and embraced them all, calling each by name. Then he spoke to Brendan.

"You have come to the Land Promised to the Saints. You could have found it long ago, but God wanted you to experience so much before you came here. You must go now, but fear not, for you will return and cross this river soon."

So Brendan and his brothers sailed away from the island and quickly reached their home in Ireland. The brothers they had left behind at the monastery welcomed them home and Brendan told them everything about their voyage, always giving thanks to the Lord.

Notes

THE GODS AND GODDESSES OF THE ANCIENT CELTS

The most important god of the Gauls: This short passage from Julius Caesar's *Gallic War* (6.17–18) is sadly our most complete list of Gaulish gods. He probably derives some of this information from the Greek Stoic philosopher Posidonius who traveled among the Gauls several decades earlier and published his observations in a work now lost. We know the names, if not always the functions, of some other Celtic gods and goddesses from ancient art and inscriptions, as well as modern archaeology. These gods include Cernunnos, the horned god of animals and nature; Ogmios, the divine poet; Matrona, the mother goddess; and Epona, the goddess of horses.

Mercury: This is almost certainly the god known across the ancient Celtic world as *Lugus,* and in medieval times as Irish *Lug* the *samildánach* ("skilled in all arts") and in Welsh as the divine craftsman *Lleu.* The ancient Irish festival of *Lughnasa* on August 1 was celebrated in honor of this most powerful and widespread Celtic god.

Apollo, Mars, Jupiter, and Minerva: In the native Gaulish and British languages these gods were sometimes called, respectively,

Belenus ("the shining one"), Caturix ("king of battle"), Taranis ("the thunderer"), and Belisama ("the brightest").

a single place: As confirmed by other ancient authors (e.g., Posidonius via Strabo, *Geography* 4.1.13) and modern archaeology, these spoils were often deposited in bodies of water, seen as gateways to the world of the gods.

THE GODS OF DARKNESS

The Gauls all say: From Julius Caesar, *Gallic War* (6.18).

Dis: Also known as Dis Pater ("father of wealth"), a Roman name for Hades or Pluto, the classical god of the underworld. In early Irish mythology, the kind and fatherly Donn ("the dark one") lived on a rocky island near the setting sun where the souls of the Irish journeyed after death.

THE TWIN GODS OF THE SEA

Historians of old: From Diodorus of Sicily, *Geography* (4.56). Diodorus is almost certainly drawing on Timaeus as his source for this story.

these two gods came to them from the sea: There are many myths of sea gods among the medieval Celts, such as the Irish *Lir* and Welsh *Llŷr.*

ANCIENT GAULISH ANIMAL MAGIC

Eudoxus says the following about the Celts: This is recorded by the second-century CE writer Aelian in his book *On Animals* (17.19).

But if someone captures one of these birds: In a story of the Irish hero Cú Chulainn, he is beaten severely after he attempts to kill birds that are in fact goddesses in animal form.

The following story told by Artemidorus: This passage is from the Greek geographer Strabo, *Geography* (4.4.6).

right wings that are partly white: As in later Irish and Welsh tales, white animals were often magical and sacred to the Celts.

THE DRUIDS AND THEIR TEACHINGS

The druids study the ways of nature: From Posidonius via Strabo, *Geography* (4.4.4–5).

fire and water will overcome the world: Many ancient religions, including Christianity, teach of a violent end to the current age of humanity. This passage is all we know about the pre-Christian Celtic view of the end of the world.

It is said that the teachings of the druids: From the *Gallic War* (6.13–14) of Julius Caesar. Although Caesar fought the Gauls and killed countless numbers of them during his long war in the middle of the first century BCE, he is more sympathetic to the druids than some other Roman writers.

WOMEN OF THE DRUIDS

The female druid: From Lampridius, *Severus Alexander* (59.5), this episode occurs when the emperor Severus Alexander was setting off to drive the Germans from Gaul in 235 CE. He was assassinated by his own troops later that same year.

While the future emperor Diocletian: From Vopiscus, *Numerian* (14). In 284 CE, many years after this incident in Gaul, Diocletian killed the assassin—named Aper, Latin for "boar"—of the emperor Numerian and became emperor himself.

On certain occasions Aurelian: From Vopiscus, *Aurelian* (43.4). Aurelian became emperor and political heir of the previous emperor Claudius in the year 270 CE. He was assassinated after ruling five years.

VISIONS FROM THE DEAD

It is often said: From Tertullian, *De Anima* (57.10).

The Nasamones: A tribe that lived in ancient Libya.

spending the night near the graves: In early Irish stories, grave mounds and ancient tombs were seen as magical entrances to the Otherworld. In the preface to the Irish *Táin Bó Cuailnge* epic, a young poet spends the night near the tomb of the hero Fergus mac Róich, who comes to him there and recounts the lost story of the *Táin*.

REINCARNATION AND REBIRTH

A teaching like that of Pythagoras: From Posidonius via Diodorus of Sicily (5.28). The famous Greek philosopher and mathematician Pythagoras (author of the Pythagorean theorem) was unusual in the classical world for teaching a belief in reincarnation.

after a certain number of years: As with many aspects of Celtic belief in reincarnation, it is unclear where souls are thought to be during their time between bodies.

The most important teaching of the druids: From Julius Caesar, *Gallic War* (6.14).

DIVINATION AND HUMAN SACRIFICE

The druids predict the future: From Posidonius via Diodorus of Sicily (5.31–32).

The Gauls are all a very religious people: From Julius Caesar, *Gallic War* (6.16).

In times not so long ago: This passage (Caesar, *Gallic War* 6.19) may be from a Celtic story heard by Posidonius or Caesar. Posidonius says elsewhere (via Athenaeus 4.154), that in times past, Celtic warriors would sometimes take pledges of gold, silver, or wine and then have their own throats cut as they lay atop their shields at great feasts.

Cruel Teutates: From the *Civil War* (1.444–46), a poem by the first-century CE Roman writer Lucan. The name Teutates means "god of the tribe." A medieval commentary on this passage claims that the victims of Teutates were plunged headfirst into a cauldron, those of Esus were hung from trees, and those sacrificed to Taranis were burned in wooden cages.

Scythian Diana: The Scythians lived in the plains of Ukraine and Russia in ancient times. They were thought by the Greeks and Romans to be excessively cruel in the worship of their gods and goddess, including the goddess of woods and hunting, known to the Greeks as Artemis and as Diana by the Romans.

MISTLETOE, SACRED PLANTS,
AND MAGICAL SNAKE EGGS

I must mention: From Pliny, *Natural History* (16.249, 24.103–104, 29.52).

The druids even get their name: The druids did not in fact derive their name from the Greeks, but from an early Celtic word *derwos* ("oak tree, strong, true") going back to an Indo-European word for oak (*deru*) that was also the ultimate origin of the Greek word *dru*. The Gaulish word *druides* probably comes from a later Celtic compound form *dru* ("oak, truth") plus the ancient root *wid-* ("to see, know"), meaning "one who knows the truth."

white bulls: As elsewhere in ancient and medieval Celtic culture, white animals were seen as sacred.

a drink made from mistletoe: Many types of mistletoe are in fact poisonous, though used as effective medicines around the world in small doses.

THE HOLY ISLAND OF WOMEN

Posidonius says: As recorded in Strabo, *Geography* (4.4.6). The Samnitae (also known as Namnetes) were a Gaulish tribe that lived on the mainland near the Loire River.

a small island in the Atlantic Ocean: A few decades before Posidonius, Artemidorus of Ephesus (recorded in the same Strabo passage) said there was an island near Britain on which sacrifices were performed for the fertility goddesses Demeter and her daughter Core (also known as Persephone).

Dionysus: Posidonius substitutes for the unknown Gaulish god the name of the Greek god of wine (Roman *Bacchus*), a divinity whose worship is frequently associated in classical literature with crazed women and bizarre, violent behavior, as in Euripides' *Bacchae*.

TWO GAULISH MAGICAL SPELLS

The Tablet of Chamalières: Both this text and the Tablet of Larzac are presented in Pierre-Yves Lambert, *La Langue Gauloise* (149–72).

Maponos: A god known in ancient Britain and related to the later divine Welsh youth Mabon.

a magical incantation of women: The Gaulish phrase here (*bnas brictom* "the magic of women") is almost identical to an Irish phrase in an early Christian prayer attributed to St. Patrick that asks for protection from "the magic of women."

the seeress: Gaulish *vidlua*, a word related to the Latin root *vid-* (as in "video") and to the later Irish name *Fedelm*, a seeress in the Irish epic *Táin Bó Cuailnge*.

daughter . . . wife . . . father . . . mother: These family terms (even the male *father*) are likely to be cultic names showing ritual relations between members of the women in the group.

THE SACRED ISLE

From here: This passage comes from a fourth-century CE poem called the *Ora Maritima* by the Roman author Avienus, but its origins probably go back to reports many centuries earlier by sailors of Carthage who explored the Atlantic coasts of Europe and Africa. The starting point mentioned here is probably the islands just off the coast of Brittany in Gaul.

The Hierni: Ancient Greek name for the Irish.

THE MAGICAL ISLANDS OF IRELAND

There is a lake in the northern part of Munster: From Gerald of Wales, *The History and Topography of Ireland* (37). Munster is a province in southwest Ireland.

There is an island on a lake in Ulster: From Gerald of Wales, *The History and Topography of Ireland* (38). Ulster is in northern Ireland. This island is traditionally located in Lough Derg in County Donegal.

IMBAS FOROSNAI: THE RITUAL OF ILLUMINATING KNOWLEDGE

Imbas forosnai: From *Cormac's Glossary* (756). The word *imbas* means "great knowledge, poetic inspiration," while *forosnai* means "shining, illuminating."

behind the door: As with much in this ritual, we don't know why certain things are done, but doorways are often seen as magical places between and connecting worlds in Celtic tradition.

then lies down to sleep: Sleep and supernatural visions are linked in many ancient cultures, including the early Celts. As seen earlier, the Greek writer Nicander of Colophon recorded that the Celts would seek visions at night by the tombs of their famous men. Gerald of Wales in his *Description of Wales* (1.16) (following passage) records that the suspiciously un-Christian gift of *awen* usually comes to Welsh seers in their sleep. But Gerald speaks more charitably of those who with God's permission leave their bodies on earth "breathing without breath, living without life" to travel to the heavens or the netherworld. In a royal Irish ritual known as the *tarbfeis*, a king was chosen by a man eating his fill of a bull, sleeping with incantations sung over him by druids, then dreaming of whoever the new king should be.

It is called imbas: The etymologies of Cormac and other medieval glossary creators are often fanciful.

teinm laída: Literally "chewing the marrow." The Irish hero Finn chewing his thumb to the marrow when he needed inspiration.

Díchetal di chennaib: Literally "an incantation from the ends." We don't know what exactly this ritual consisted of or why the Christian church considered it nonthreatening enough to allow.

a telling from the ends of the bones: Again, the meaning of this is unknown.

AWEN: THE WELSH GIFT OF MAGICAL INSPIRATION

There is a certain group: From Gerald of Wales, *Description of Wales* (1.16).

with many riddles: Similar to the description of the ancient Celts of Gaul (Diodorus of Sicily 5.31): "They are a people of few words and often speak in riddles, leaving many things for the listener to understand."

Because of similar events in ancient writings and the Christian scriptures: This is a summary of several previous paragraphs in this chapter in which Gerald lists both classical and biblical precedents for inspiration and prophecy, as well as the Arthurian wizard Merlin.

THE IRISH STORY OF CREATION

In the beginning God: This short selection is condensed from the beginning of the Irish *Lebor Gabála Érenn* (*The Book of Invasions*).

THE REINCARNATIONS OF TUÁN SON OF CAIRELL

One day a Christian holy man: The original Irish story of Tuán, *Scél Tuáin meic Chairill,* is edited by John Carey.

the Ulaid: The people of Ulster in northeast Ireland.

the gods and un-gods: Literally the *tuatha dé ocus an-dé,* a peculiar and mysterious phrase.

Sons of Míl . . . Tuatha dé Danaan: As seen in the following two stories.

THE COMING OF THE TUATHA DÉ DANAAN

Many people came to Ireland: The story presented here comes from several sources, primarily *Cath Maige Tuired,* edited by Elizabeth Grey.

the Lia Fáil: Also known as the Stone of Destiny, it has a long and colorful history. The stone stands even today on the Hill of Tara, the ancient seat of Irish kings in modern County Meath, north of Dublin.

THE SONGS OF AMAIRGEN

When the Tuatha Dé Danaan: From the *Lebor Gabála Érenn* (*The Book of Invasions*).

THE TAKING OF THE *SÍD* MOUND

There was once a wondrous king: From the Irish *De Gabáil in t-Sída* (*The Taking of the Síd*).

THE ADVENTURES OF NERA IN THE OTHERWORLD

On the cold, dark night of Samain: From the Irish story *Echtrae Nera* (*The Adventures of Nera*).

Ailill and Medb: Frequent characters in Irish stories, including the epic *Táin Bó Cuailgne,* they were the king and queen of the western Irish province of Connacht.

the nearby cave of Cruachan: This cave exists near the remains of Cruachan in County Roscommon. Archaeologists have found evidence that it was an active religious site stretching back deep into prehistory.

THE LIVES OF ÉTAÍN

The king of the Tuatha Dé Danaan: From the Irish story *Tochmarc Étaíne* ("The Wooing of Étaín").

to be fostered: It was common in medieval Ireland for children of the nobility to be given to foster parents to be raised, as a way of strengthening communities and building alliances.

all of time is made of a day and a night: This is the same trick played on the Dagda himself in the earlier story, "The Taking of the *Síd* Mound."

Ailill: Not the same king as in *The Adventures of Nera.*

your first wife, Fuamnach: According to ancient Irish law, a senior wife was allowed to beat a new wife for three days.

fidchell: A board game like chess popular in medieval Ireland.

THE STORY OF THE SHANNON RIVER

How did the shining Shannon River: From the medieval Irish tradition known as the *Dinnshenchas Erenn* (*Placenames of Ireland*).

Well of Connla: Not the same as the Connla in the next story, the origin of this figure is unknown. But the Well of Connla occurs in several early Irish stories as a source of Otherworld wisdom, similar to the magical Well of Mímir in Norse mythology.

Salmon would then come: As in the Irish story of Finn and the Welsh tale of Taliesin, salmon were often the bearers of inspired wisdom in Celtic mythology.

CONNLA AND THE WOMAN OF THE OTHERWORLD

Connla of the Red Hair: From the Irish *Echtrae Conli* (*The Adventures of Connla*).

Uisnech: An ancient ceremonial site in modern County Westmeath near the geographic center of Ireland. It was traditionally held to be the sacred, spiritual heart of the island.

THE BOYHOOD DEEDS OF FINN

There was once a war: From the Irish story *Macgnímartha Finn* (*The Boyhood Deeds of Finn*).

Slieve Bloom: A mountain range in central Ireland.

finn: The Irish word for "fair, bright."

teinm laída: As seen in the earlier ritual of the *imbas forosnai, teinm laída* means "chewing the marrow."

the Paps of Anu: Two large, round hills in County Kerry shaped like giant breasts. Anu (or Ana) was one of the mother goddesses of Ireland.

the women of the síd: In Irish, an Otherworld woman (*ban*) of the fairy mound (*síd*) gives rise to the English word *banshee*, a supernatural female known for wailing and keening.

THE STORY OF GWION BACH AND TALIESIN

In the days when King Arthur: From the medieval Welsh *Hanes Taliesin* (*The Tale of Taliesin*).

THE ANCIENT IRISH HORSE SACRIFICE

There are some things I am: From Gerald of Wales, *The History and Topography of Ireland,* (102).

Kenelcunill: The Tír Chonaill tribe of what is now County Donegal.

a white mare: As seen earlier, white animals were often associated with the gods and divine world in Celtic mythology.

THE CONFESSION OF ST. PATRICK

My name is Patrick: The seven surviving Latin medieval manuscripts of Patrick's letters are edited by Ludwig Bieler in *Libri Epistolarum Sancti Patricii Episcopi.*

a deacon of the church: An ordained Christian minister who performed many functions in the early church, but served at a lower rank than a priest, such as Patrick's grandfather.

Bannaventa Berniae: This is the most reasonable reconstruction of a name that is garbled in the surviving manuscripts. We don't know where in Roman Britain it was, but it seems reasonable that it was near the western coast close to the Irish Sea.

Listen as I declare my faith: Patrick is clearly concerned in this letter to show that he is an orthodox Christian and so gives us here a statement very similar, though abbreviated, of the Nicene and other early creeds endorsed by church authorities.

how limited my education is: Patrick was kidnapped from Britain just before he would have begun the final phase of education for a young Roman nobleman. His Latin is good enough to express himself, but he is painfully aware that it lacks the polish and rhetorical skills found in the writings of most Christian bishops.

two hundred miles away: Roman miles, the equivalent of about 180 modern miles. Since Ireland is small, this means that Patrick crossed almost the entire island to escape.

I refused to suck their breasts: A Latin phrase (*sugere mammellas*) so odd it was deliberately changed in many of the early manuscripts, though it is almost certainly what Patrick wrote and refers to an initiation ritual mentioned elsewhere in medieval Irish literature.

wandered about lost in an empty land: In his letters Patrick is fond of using biblical language and images of Israelites escaping from slavery in Egypt.

feeding their dogs: These may have been part of the ship's cargo, since enormous Irish dogs were exported to Roman lands.

to call on Elijah: An episode playing on the similarity of the name of the Hebrew prophet Elijah (Latin *Helias*) with the classical sun god *Helios,* popular in the late Roman empire. Elijah was a frequent figure of art and invocation in the early Christian church.

Victoricus: A Roman name, perhaps a fellow captive in Ireland.

the woods of Voclut: Presumably the place where Patrick was enslaved, probably in County Mayo.

a sin I had committed more than thirty years earlier: Patrick never explains what this sin was, but it must have been very serious to cause him trouble when revealed decades later.

virgins of Christ: There is no reason to doubt the sincerity of these Christian women to follow God and abstain from sexual relations, but there was also a profound sense of freedom for those who removed themselves from a patriarchal system of marriage alliances that was central to Irish society. This helps to explain the anger of the fathers toward the daughters who vowed to be virgins for Christ.

the slave women: In Irish society, slavery was even harsher than among the Romans. Enslaved men and women were treated as mere property and could not buy their freedom, as they often could in the Roman world.

ST. PATRICK'S LETTER TO THE SOLDIERS OF COROTICUS

My name is Patrick: From Ludwig Bieler, *Libri Epistolarum Sancti Patricii Episcopi.*

THE FIRST SYNOD OF ST. PATRICK

Christians should not attempt: The Latin text of the First Synod of St. Patrick is edited by M. J. Faris in *The Bishops' Synod.*

If a priest wanders about naked: The native Irish were apparently less prudish about the human body than the Christian missionaries who came to the island. The standard hairstyle for a Roman-approved priest or monk was to shave just the top of the head. Married priests were common in the early church with celibacy not becoming the rule in Western Europe until the late Middle Ages.

lamia: A female monster or witch that sucked the blood of children at night.

THE IRISH PENITENTIALS

These selections are all from the *Penitential of Cummean,* edited by Ludwig Bieler in *The Irish Penitentials.*

THE LEGENDS OF ST. PATRICK

In the days of holy Patrick: From Muirchu, *Life of St. Patrick,* edited by Ludwig Bieler in *The Patrician Texts of the Book of Armagh.*

A man with a shaved head will come: This refers to Patrick's tonsure as a monk, whereas the bent stick is his bishop's staff. He sings Christian hymns in his church and celebrates the mass at the table in front, while his people reply *Amen* ("Let it be so").

a contest of miracles: This is based on the biblical stories of the magicians who contested with Moses before the pharaoh and the battle between Elijah and the prophets of the god Baal.

smelled as sweet as honey: A common feature in the stories of medieval saints after their death.

THE GODDESSES BRIGID

Brigid—a poetess and daughter: From *Sanas Cormaic* (*Cormac's Glossary*), 150.

the Dagda: the king of the divine Tuatha Dé Danaan, whose name means "the good god."

THE LIFE OF ST. BRIGID

Holy Brigid was born in Ireland: These stories of Brigid are abbreviated selections from the Latin life of the saint written by an Irish churchman named Cogitosus in the seventh century. I have translated and taken selections of the story from medieval Latin manuscripts from libraries in England, France, Germany, Belgium, and Italy.

Her father's name was Dubthach: Another early source says Brigid's mother was a slave and her father a druid.

turned the water into the finest beer: Beer was much more common in Ireland than wine, as in the story from the wedding at Cana in the Bible on which this miracle is based.

the fetus inside of her disappeared: There is another early Irish story in which a saint named Ciarán blesses the womb of a nun who has been raped and makes the fetus inside her vanish.

a valuable silver brooch: In early Irish law, a person could be reduced to slavery if they didn't pay a debt.

Kildare: Meaning "the church of the oak," it was the monastic community for men and women founded by Brigid west of modern Dublin.

THE HOLY FIRE OF ST. BRIGID

Kildare in Leinster: From Gerald of Wales, *History and Topography of Ireland* (2.67–68).

THE LIFE OF ST. DARERCA

There was once a virgin named Darerca: From the medieval Latin *Life of St. Darerca.*

the tribe of the Conaille: Located in County Louth, north-central Ireland.

Mag Coba: In County Down, southeast of modern Belfast.

St. Ibar: Traditionally one of the missionaries to Ireland who arrived before St. Patrick.

Leinster: Southeast Ireland. Brigid's church was at Kildare.

ST. COLUMBA AND THE LOCH NESS MONSTER

On one occasion blessed Columba: From Adomnán, *Life of St. Columba.*

the land of the Picts: The Picts were probably a Celtic people who lived in what is now Scotland during Roman times and for several centuries after. Beginning in the fifth century of the Christian era, they began to be displaced by Gaelic-speaking immigrants from Ireland known as the *Scotti*, who gave their name to modern Scotland.

CHRISTIAN IRISH POETRY

Composed in the margins of manuscripts by Irish monks far from home, the texts of the two poems are edited by Whitley Stokes and John Strachan in *Thesaurus Paleohibernicus*, vol. 2 (290, 293–94).

THE VOYAGE OF BRAN

One day Bran: From the medieval Irish story *The Voyage of Bran,* edited by Kuno Meyer.

THE VOYAGE OF ST. BRENDAN

Holy Brendan, son of Findlug: From the medieval Latin story *Navigatio Sancti Brendani Abbatis,* edited by Carl Selmer.

Further Reading

Aldhouse-Green, Miranda. *The Celtic Myths: A Guide to the Ancient Gods and Legends.* London: Thames and Hudson, 2015.

Bergin, Osborn, and R. I. Best. "Tochmarc Étaíne," *Ériu* 12 (1938, 137–96).

Bieler, Ludwig. *The Irish Penitentials.* Dublin: Dublin Institute for Advanced Studies, 1975.

———. *The Patrician Texts of the Book of Armagh.* Dublin: Dublin Institute for Advanced Studies, 1979.

———. *Libri Epistolarum Sancti Patricii Episcopi.* Dublin: Royal Irish Academy, 1993.

Carey, John. "Scél Tuáin meic Chairill," *Ériu* 35 (1984, 93–111).

Cunliffe, Barry. *The Ancient Celts.* New York: Penguin, 1997.

Davies, Oliver, and Thomas O'Loughlin. *Celtic Spirituality.* New York: Paulist Press, 1999.

De Paor, Liam. *Saint Patrick's World.* Notre Dame: University of Notre Dame Press, 1993.

Faris, M. J., ed. *The Bishops' Synod.* Liverpool: Francis Cairns, 1976.

Ford, Patrick. *The Mabinogi and Other Medieval Welsh Tales.* Berkeley: University of California Press, 2008.

Freeman, Philip. *War, Women, and Druids: Eyewitness Reports and Early Accounts of the Ancient Celts.* Austin: University of Texas Press, 2002.

————. *The Philosopher and the Druids: A Journey Among the Ancient Celts,* Simon & Schuster, 2006.

————. *The World of Saint Patrick.* New York: Oxford University Press, 2014.

————. *Celtic Mythology.* New York: Oxford University Press, 2017.

Gantz, Jeffery. *Early Irish Myths and Sagas.* New York: Penguin, 1981.

Green, Miranda. *The World of the Druids.* London: Thames and Hudson, 1997.

Grey, Elizabeth, ed. *Cath Maige Tuired.* Dublin: Irish Texts Society, 1982.

Jackson, Kenneth. *A Celtic Miscellany.* New York: Penguin, 1971.

Kinsella, Thomas. *The Táin.* Oxford: Oxford University Press, 1969.

Koch, John, and John Carey. *The Celtic Heroic Age.* Aberystwyth, Wales: Celtic Studies Publications, 2003.

Lambert, Pierre-Yves. *La Langue Gauloise.* Paris: Editions Errance, 1994.

Macalister, R. A. Stewart. *The Book of Invasions.* London: Irish Texts Society, 1993.

Mac Cana, Proinsias. *Celtic Mythology.* New York: Peter Bedrick Books, 1983.

MacKillop, James. *Dictionary of Celtic Mythology.* Oxford: Oxford University Press, 1998.

MacLeod, Sharon Price. *Celtic Myth and Religion.* Jefferson, North Carolina: McFarland and Company, 2012.

Meyer, Kuno. *The Voyage of Bran.* London: David Nutt, 1895.

———. "Boyish Exploits of Finn," *Ériu* 1 (1904, 180–90).

Nagy, Joseph. *The Wisdom of the Outlaw*. Berkeley: University of California Press, 1985.

O'Donohue, John. *Anam Ċara: A Book of Celtic Wisdom*. New York: HarperCollins, 1997.

O'Loughlin, Thomas. *Celtic Theology*. London: Continuum, 2000.

O'Meara, John. *The Voyage of Saint Brendan*. Buckinghamshire: Colin Smythe, 1991.

O'Rahilly, Cecile. *Táin Bó Cuailgne: Recension I*. Dublin: Dublin Institute for Advanced Studies, 1976.

Raftery, Barry. *Pagan Celtic Ireland*. London: Thames and Hudson, 1994.

Selmer, Carl. *Navigatio Sancti Brendani Abbatis*. Dublin: Four Courts Press, 1989.

Stokes, Whitley, and John Strachan. *Thesaurus Paleohibernicus*, vol. 2. Dublin: Dublin Institute for Advanced Studies, 1975.

About the Author

Pepperdine University Photo Office

Philip Freeman earned a Ph.D. from Harvard University and currently holds an endowed chair in humanities at Pepperdine University in Malibu, California. He has published more than twenty books on ancient and medieval history and religion, including works on Celtic mythology and St. Patrick.